A CREATIVE STEP-BY-STEP GUIDE TO

FLOWERING
SHRUBS & TREES

A CREATIVE STEP-BY-STEP GUIDE TO

FLOWERING
SHRUBS & TREES

Author
Sue Phillips

Photographer
Neil Sutherland

Colour
Library

4537
Published in 1997 by Colour Library Direct
© 1997 CLB International, Godalming, Surrey
Printed and bound in Singapore
ISBN 1-85833-584-1

Credits

Edited, designed and typeset by Ideas into Print
Photographs: Neil Sutherland
Production Director: Gerald Hughes
Production: Ruth Arthur, Neil Randles, Paul Randles,
Janine Seddon, Karen Staff

THE AUTHOR

Sue Phillips began gardening at the age of four, encouraged by her grandfather, and had her first greenhouse at eleven, where she grew a collection of cacti and propagated all sorts of plants. After leaving school, she worked for a year on a general nursery before studying horticulture at Hadlow College of Agriculture & Horticulture, Kent for three years. For the next five years, she was co-owner and manager of a nursery in Cambridgeshire, before joining a leading garden products company as Gardens Adviser. This involved answering gardening queries, handling complaints, writing articles and press releases, speaking at gardening events and broadcasting for local radio. In 1984, she turned freelance and since then she has contributed regularly to various gardening and general interest magazines and has appeared often on radio and TV. She is the author of several published books. She lives in a very windy village on the south coast of England near Chichester and has a very intensively cultivated cottage garden on solid clay, plus a vegetable garden next door, which she looks after with help from her husband and hindrance from a Persian cat.

THE PHOTOGRAPHER

Neil Sutherland has more than 25 years experience in a wide range of photographic fields, including still-life, portraiture, reportage, natural history, cookery, landscape and travel. His work has been published in countless books and magazines throughout the world.

Half-title page: Magnolia liliiflora 'Nigra'.
Title page: Buddleia flowers in a range of forms and colors.
Copyright page: The elegant and fragrant flowers of Hamamelis *x* intermedia 'Vezna' *in a winter garden.*

CONTENTS

THE HEART OF ANY GARDEN

Flowering shrubs and trees are deservedly the most popular of plants. They are the heart of any garden and you could make a complete garden using nothing else. They represent superb value for money, since they live, grow and flower for many years, demand little in return, yet cost less - size for size - than herbaceous flowers. A huge range of popular flowering shrubs and trees are available, which makes it easy to find something to suit every garden situation. Shrubs team up well with each other to make a border of their own, but also look lovely grown as the backdrop for a mixed planting of other shrubs and flowers, underplanted with bulbs. A mixture of evergreens and deciduous kinds ensures interest all the year round. If the border is big enough, large shrubs can be accompanied by a tree or two in the back row. In a small garden, complement a pretty border with a single well-shaped specimen tree in the middle of a lawn. Many shrubs are dual-purpose, suitable for training as either large shrubs or small trees, or as either wall shrubs or free-standing bushy plants. And since they need little attention, shrubs and trees form the ideal basis for an easy-care garden. By planting through a plastic mulch covered with decorative gravel or chippings, even chores such as weeding can be eliminated. This book shows you how easy it is to choose, plant and care for some of the most popular flowering shrubs and trees, to make your garden more vibrant, colorful and ever-changing throughout the seasons.

Left: A path through rhododendrons and other shrubs and trees.   *Right:* Hypericum *x* moserianum *'Tricolor'.*

Making the most of your soil

Good garden soil does not usually just happen; it takes several years of regular cultivation to create, and most gardeners need to include soil improvement in their day-to-day garden routine. This happens in several stages. First, whenever you make a new bed or border, dig in plenty of well-rotted organic matter, such as garden compost or composted manure, into the whole area, burying it to the full depth of the spade. Use about a barrowload per square meter; you will need more on light sandy or chalky soils. Then each time you add a new plant, dig a bucketful of organic matter into the bottom of the planting hole. Finally, spread a mulch over the soil surface. This not only looks decorative, but also traps moisture in the soil and smothers out weed seedlings. Reapply mulches each spring (or spring and fall on very dry sandy or chalky soils). If low maintenance is your aim, spread a decorative layer of a long-lasting surface mulch of gravel or bark chippings over a carpet of slitted black plastic, (often sold as landscape fabric), which totally prevents weeds.

Improving the soil

Due to the special characteristics of organic matter, the same materials can be used to open up heavy soils and improve their aeration and drainage, and improve moisture retention in dry sandy or chalky soils. Dig in organic soil improvers, such as well-rotted garden compost or horse manure, coir or moss peat, before planting, fork them in between established plants or use them as a surface mulch.

TYPES OF SOIL
These are the main types of soil found in gardens; each one can be improved with soil conditioners and by feeding and mulching to make good conditions for growing a wide range of plants.

Chalky soils look pale, with a whitish cast if chalk rock is present. There may be particles of pure chalk. Pale soil may cover a layer of chalk rock lower down. The soil is very alkaline, fast-draining and low in nutrients, which are locked up chemically.

Clay soil forms hard clods in summer, when cracks often appear in the soil. When wet, the soil is sticky and a handful forms a ball that holds its shape. In the garden, soil stays wet and puddles take ages to disappear.

Sandy soil is usually light buff to orange-brown in color. Water runs through it very quickly, so that puddles vanish immediately after rain and a handful of damp soil will not hold together in a ball when squeezed.

Good garden soil is a deep, rich loam, dark in color due to the organic matter added over several years of regular cultivation. It holds moisture, but is never boggy.

Woodland soils contain large amounts of leaf mold in various stages of decomposition. They are usually slightly acid, rich and fertile, and hold moisture. Plentiful air spaces allow surplus moisture to drain away freely.

MULCHES

A mulch is a layer of material spread over the soil surface to 'seal' moisture into the soil, smother out annual weeds, and give a decorative finish.

Cocoa shell chips are slightly acid and break down quickly. Apply annually to damp soil in early spring. They deter cats and slugs.

Gravel is a good surface for dry gardens or over landscape fabric for a low-maintenance garden. Top up occasionally.

Chipped bark, a long-lasting mulch, is ideal for shrub borders. Top it up every few years.

Soil testing kits

Cheap soil testing kits are available in garden centers. They are easy to use and give a result within minutes. For best results, do several tests using soil from different places round the garden as soils can vary within a small area.

1 With this type of kit, put a little dry soil into the tube, up to the level indicated. Add water to the next mark on the side of the tube, replace the cap and shake well.

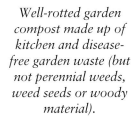

2 When the water changes color, compare it to the chart provided to see if your soil is acid, neutral or alkaline. From this you can determine which kinds of plants will suit it.

SOIL IMPROVERS

Moss peat is naturally acidic with a spongy texture. Use it to acidify neutral or slightly acid soil before planting acid-loving plants.

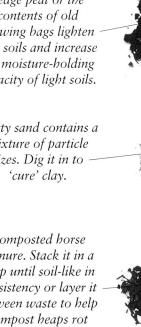

Well-rotted garden compost made up of kitchen and disease-free garden waste (but not perennial weeds, weed seeds or woody material).

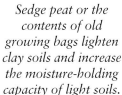

Sedge peat or the contents of old growing bags lighten clay soils and increase the moisture-holding capacity of light soils.

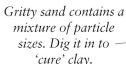

Gritty sand contains a mixture of particle sizes. Dig it in to 'cure' clay.

Composted horse manure. Stack it in a heap until soil-like in consistency or layer it between waste to help compost heaps rot down faster.

Coir. Use it alone as a soil improver or in the form of ready-made sowing and potting mixtures.

Conditioning the soil

Before starting to plant a new garden, it is a good idea to discover whether your soil is acid, neutral or alkaline, as this will influence the types of plants that will grow well in it. Then use the appropriate soil additives and improvers to condition it. The aim is to turn a soil that may only have supported rather specialized plants (e.g. those that tolerate starved or perhaps very chalky conditions) into one in which a much wider range of normal garden plants will thrive.

Calcified seaweed breaks down clay soils and neutralizes acid ones. A source of magnesium, calcium and trace elements.

Sulfur chips acidify a neutral or slightly alkaline soil.

General purpose fertilizers restore the soil's major nutrients.

Choosing shrubs and trees

When choosing garden trees and shrubs, most people buy on impulse, picking whatever takes their fancy from the plants in flower. But some plants need particular conditions and it is all too easy to get them home, only to find that you have nowhere suitable to put them. Worse still, you plant them in the wrong spot and they do not grow. Plants need matching to the situations where they are to grow. This is why it is essential to know your garden: the soil type and whether it is acid, alkaline or neutral, and which areas are in full sun, partial or total shade at given times of the day. Then by planting the right plants in the right places, they will be able to do their best. Nowadays, most garden centers and nurseries provide full information about the individual preferences of each plant they sell. Most popular shrubs and trees will grow in any reasonable garden soil, but some plants are useful for particular 'problem' places. But always start by choosing the best-quality plants you can find. They will perform well from the start; much better than waiting for second best plants to catch up.

Many shrubs, such as this Chaenomeles, can be grown as free-standing bushes or trained flat against a wall.

Plants that are already wall-trained are much more expensive to buy. This is Camellia x williamsii *'Donation'.*

Rhododendrons need acid soil, shelter and light, dappled shade. Being shallow-rooted, they need soil that stays moist in summer, so a good leafy woodland soil is ideal.

Ribes grows in any reasonable garden soil (a term that covers a wide range of garden conditions excluding only the extremes), in full sun or light shade.

Choosing a plant

Always choose a neat, bushy specimen, with plenty of shoots and a symmetrical shape. Avoid plants with yellow leaves; they may be half-starved or have dried out. These, and plants that need remedial pruning, will take time to recover. Buying a plant in flower means you can be sure that it is the correct variety.

BAD PLANT
Avoid leggy plants with bare stems and dead shoots, indicating previous neglect.

GOOD PLANT
A good plant has a neat, compact and symmetrical shape, with leaves to the base.

Pieris *is a good evergreen shrub for acid soil and light, dappled shade. If kept moist enough it will grow in sun.*

Choisya ternata '*Sundance*' *makes a dense, compact, small evergreen shrub with good foliage, suitable for all-year-round planting in a tub.*

Above: *Choose trees with a straight trunk, free from tiny side-shoots, and several well placed branches radiating out evenly to form a good 'head'. Check the ultimate size - many grow too big for small gardens.*

Brooms are some of the best plants to grow in an exposed situation with poor dry soil, conditions that are too harsh for many plants to succeed in.

Planting a small tree

Having spent what is often a fairly hefty sum on a tree, do not be tempted to economize when it comes to planting it; a properly planted tree is far more likely to survive and go on to perform well. Start by improving the soil. If the bed is new, dig plenty of well-rotted organic matter deeply into the whole area first. If you are planting into an existing, well-cultivated bed, simply dig out a planting hole about twice the size of the tree's rootball. Fork a bucketful of well-rotted organic matter into the bottom and add some more to the soil used to fill in round the roots, together with a sprinkling of any good-quality general fertilizer, following the maker's instructions. This is necessary because today's plants are grown in potting mixture that is so different from garden soil that roots are often disinclined to grow out into it when planted, hence plants fail. By improving the soil and teasing out a few potbound roots, new plants are able to colonize the surrounding soil with young roots. They quickly become established and grow away freely. The technique of planting shown here is the same for shrubs as for trees, except that shrubs do not need staking.

3 Dig a planting hole larger than the tree's rootball, hammer a short stake in to one side of it, then plant so that the top of the rootball is roughly flush with the soil surface when the hole is filled in.

1 Remove the tree from its container. Plants lift out easily from rigid plastic pots. In the case of plastic bag-type pots, slit the sides with a knife, taking care not to cut through the roots; then lift out.

2 If there are any suckers arising from the base, scrape back the soil to expose their junction with a root and tear or cut them out from there. Snipping off the top makes the problem worse.

4 Firm the soil down well with your boot to make sure that there are no air pockets left in it. These would leave roots hanging in space, where they tend to dry out and die, instead of making contact with the soil.

5 Water well in after planting, even if the soil is already moist; this helps wash the soil well down around the roots. If the soil sinks, add more to bring it back to the correct level.

6 While the soil is still wet, scatter about 2in(5cm) of good mulching material over it. Coarse bark chippings have been used here. This helps to retain moisture in the soil and also suppresses weed growth.

7 Secure the tree trunk to the stake with a proper tree tie, positioned just below the lowest branches. Make sure the 'buffer' is correctly placed between the stake and the trunk to prevent the bark chafing in the wind.

Staking a tree

When planting a tree, do not overdo the staking. Nowadays it has been found that trees 'learn' to support themselves better with only a short stake, left in place for a year or two after planting. This is enough to stop the roots being rocked loose in the soil in windy weather, whilst allowing the top of the trunk to flex. Trees then develop strengthening fibers that will support them when the stakes are removed. Trees with very small or weak root systems, such as apple and crab apple trees growing on very dwarfing rootstocks, will need the support of a stake throughout their lives. This should reach to the level of the lowest branches.

8 Keep new trees watered during dry spells to help them establish. This is specially important if the tree is planted during spring or summer, when there is little natural rainfall to take care of the job. Remove the stake after a year or two.

Amelanchier

Very few trees are both compact enough for small gardens and have enough year-round appeal to justify the space they take up, but one of the best is the snowy mespilus *(Amelanchier lamarckii)*. This hardy and tolerant tree grows to about 12ft(3.7m) high and the same across. Its season starts in spring, when the sprays of warm-white blossom coincide with the arrival of the bronze young foliage fresh from newly burst buds. Later, the tree is studded with red fruit, which proves a great attraction to visiting birds. (This makes *Amelanchier* a good tree for a wildlife garden.) In the fall, the leaves take on vivid tints and hang on for quite some time. Yet even in winter, *Amelanchier* has a fine mushroomlike shape, with a dense twiggy outline that makes it a permanent feature of the landscape. *Amelanchier* can also be grown as a large bushy shrub; this may happen accidentally if the head of the tree is broken after planting, in which case strong shoots arise from the remains of the trunk. (Snowy mespilus is not grafted, so suckers are the original tree, not those of a rootstock.) You can grow your own bush amelanchier from suckers arising from the base of a mature tree or raise seed or natural-sown seedlings. Nip out the tip when it is a few inches high to encourage branching. Once the basic shape of either the tree or bush are formed (usually done at the nursery before you buy the plant) there is no need for any pruning, other than removing damaged branches.

Growing conditions

Amelanchiers are one of the least fussy yet most reliable trees. They tolerate a wide range of soils, from slightly chalky to quite acid, and from rather dry to quite wet. They even do well on clay soils that are wet in winter and dry out badly in summer (though it is advisable to water well for the first summer to help a new tree get established in dry soil). Give amelanchiers full or partial sun, otherwise flowering and fall color will be less good.

Above: The most commonly grown amelanchier, A. lamarckii, is especially striking in spring, when the coppery-bronze young foliage creates a rich background for the off-white blossom.

Left: The berries of amelanchier are a favorite midsummer food for birds. The berries are harmless to humans; in fact the red berries of A. canadensis, shown here, were once used as food.

Right: Amelanchier produces a final fiery flourish in the fall. Its color is much more reliable than that of many other trees, which are more dependent on particular weather conditions.

Left: *Amelanchiers can also be grown as large bushes, simply by asking the nursery to save you an untrimmed plant. Alternatively, grow your own from a sucker taken from around the base of an older tree.*

Right: *Amelanchier flowers are small and starlike, but very wind resistant. They therefore last a long time in good condition before falling, unlike those of many spring trees, such as lilacs and flowering cherry.*

Berberis

Berberis form a large group of easy-to-grow, mid-spring to early summer-flowering shrubs with bunches of orange or yellow flowers. They grow happily in most soils and situations, from full sun to shade, and are some of the few plants that - once established - thrive in dry shade under large trees. The only thing berberis do not much care for is waterlogged roots. Both deciduous and evergreen kinds make good background shrubs for a mixed border, where they associate well with smaller shrubs, flowers and bulbs. Berberis are all prickly - some aggressively so - and the branches interlock; these factors combine to produce very dense, impenetrable hedges and intruder-repellent borders. Berberis hedges are fully clothed right to the base, preventing animals getting into - or out of - the garden. They also trap flying litter, dust from traffic, dead leaves and other debris, thus helping to keep the garden tidy. As well as the better known large to medium-sized kinds suitable for beds, borders or boundaries, there are also compact cultivars suitable for growing on banks or raised beds and rock gardens, and a few that make good specimen plants. There are also some berberis with very striking colored or variegated foliage, in shades of gold, pink, mauve, red and purple. Although these are not always the best cultivars for floral display, the combination of flowers and foliage makes more of a spectacle and the foliage continues to act as a background for other plants and flowers all through the summer. Some species produce interesting crops of berries in late summer; barberry jam was once made from the fruit of *Berberis vulgaris*.

The green, dome-shaped Berberis thunbergii *'Kobold' is a deciduous dwarf form with good fall color. Ideal for rock gardens or other small spaces.*

Berberis linearifolia 'Jewel'

Berberis 'Goldilocks'

Left: *The yellow, knobbly flowers of* Berberis *'Goldilocks' look like tiny bunches of grapes.* Berberis linearifolia *'Jewel' produces a mass of orange flowers. Both these attractive, but uncommon, cultivars flower in early spring, long before most other berberis.*

Left: B. stenophylla, *one of the most popular and readily available species, makes a medium to large prickly bush. This cultivar is 'Etna', a very prolific and brightly colored form.*

Right: *Berberis thunbergii 'Atropurpurea Nana' remains small, dense and compact, which makes it ideal for growing on rock gardens, at the front of a border or in raised beds. The autumn-like coloration is carried throughout the season, but the leaves are shed in the fall.*

Rejuvenating berberis

Old, woody berberis shrubs can be rejuvenated over a period of several years by cutting out a few of the thickest old branches at ground level each spring. This encourages plenty of new shoots to spring up from the base of the plant; in the colored-leaved cultivars this new growth has the best coloration. After pruning, apply a generous mulch of organic matter and sprinkle a handful of general fertilizer over the area around the plants. Normally, berberis - especially the evergreen kinds - keep a neat shape without any pruning.

Berberis thunbergii 'Harlequin', *a deciduous, medium-sized, bushy shrub, is grown for its loud pink-variegated-purple foliage.*

Berberis stenophylla 'Claret Cascade' *makes quite a large prickly evergreen shrub. All three varieties flower in late spring to early summer.*

Left: *The oldest stems of a mature berberis are thick with branching from the top, while young shoots are thin and bendy, with foliage to the base. Here, the oldest stem is being removed from an old B. thunbergii atropurpurea.*

Below: *A long shoot may sometimes spoil the shape of the plant. Snip these off whenever you see them, at any time of year.*

Buddleia - the butterfly bush

Once its few needs are provided for, buddleia puts on a wonderful display in mid- to late summer, when its long, conical flowers in white, purple, mauve and lilac shades come alive with butterflies almost from the moment they open. Buddleia is a wonderfully adaptable shrub that tolerates salt, wind and pollution, and poor dry soil. In gardens, buddleia needs a sunny situation with reasonably well-drained soil to thrive. Even when correctly pruned, buddleia grows about 10ft(3m) tall and 6ft(1.8m) across, so use it at the back of a border behind other shrubs or flowers, or in a wildlife garden as a specimen shrub to attract butterflies. It is also a useful shrub for a 'problem' dry sunny bank, or in poor, rubble-filled soil. Although *Buddleia davidii*, described here, is by far the most popular buddleia, other species are sometimes seen in nurseries.

Pruning a mature buddleia

The butterfly bush (Buddleia davidii) *is a common enough sight in gardens, but how often do you see a really well-grown and cared-for specimen? The trick lies mainly in pruning, but a spring mulch and regular feeding (page 12) also pay dividends. Just a little of the right attention can transform this popular plant.*

1 *A neglected buddleia will consist of a lot of thick, woody old stems 6ft(1.8m) high or more. In mid-spring, use a pruning saw to cut these down to about 2ft(60cm) from the ground.*

2 *The best flowers are produced at the tips of young stems, and hard pruning brings the flowers down to a height where you can see them.*

B. d. 'Harlequin' *is the only buddleia with variegated foliage. It looks good when not in flower, but often flowers a bit less profusely than normal green kinds.*

B. d. 'Nanho Blue'. *All the Nanho varieties grow rather smaller than most buddleias, to about 6ft(1.8m) high in a growing season instead of 8-10ft(2.5-3m).*

Buddleia x weyeriana *has ball-shaped clusters of yellow-orange flowers. Provide a sheltered site and rich soil.*

Buddleia fallowiana, *one of the species buddleias, has slightly silvery-white woolly stems and leaves. It needs a sheltered position.*

Pruning new buddleia

When you buy a buddleia plant in spring, it may or may not have been pruned. Pruning it will encourage new shoots to start growing straight away. If you buy a buddleia in late spring or summer do not prune it until the following year or you lose the current year's flowers. Once planted, prune the buddleia every year in spring, cutting it back to about 2ft(60cm) each time.

Left: An unpruned plant is tall and lanky and carries the remains of the previous year's dead flowerheads. A pruned plant quickly puts on new growth and gets off to a good start.

1 Cut an unpruned plant down to about 6in(15cm) from the top of the pot with secateurs before planting. Cut just above a strong young shoot.

2 Repeat the same process with each stem until the whole plant is only a few inches tall, with a mass of new shoots visible at the top.

3 Each year, cut back the top one third of the plant after flowering in late summer. Then prune each spring, but only cutting back to 2ft(60cm).

Buddleia lindleyana 'Lochinch' grows 6ft(1.8m) high and 4ft(1.2m) across. It needs well-drained soil and full sun.

B. officinalis 'Pink Delight' is a newer variety. It has a good bright color and similar temperament to B.d. 'Black Knight'.

B. davidii 'Black Knight' is widely available, very tough and tolerant of most soils. It is especially attractive to butterflies.

Above: Buddleia x weyeriana *makes a large dense shrub, ideal for the back of a sunny border or as a specimen plant in the lawn. It needs no pruning.*

Right: *The unusual B. alternifolia is generally trained as a small tree with cascading branches. If grown as a bush, it makes an untidy, floppy shape.*

Camellias

Camellias are one of the most popular spring-flowering evergreens. In mild winters, cultivars of *Camellia* x *williamsii* often flower sporadically from late fall onwards, given a well sheltered spot. *C. japonica* cultivars can take a few years to begin blooming when first planted, but are worth waiting for. They need deadheading, as the flowers tend to hang on the stems when they are over. Camellia flowers come in various forms: singles, doubles, semi-doubles and some with very formal, rosettelike flowers. There are also water lily shapes and anemone-centered blooms. Pink and red camellias are generally the most reliable - white flowers tend to turn brown if the weather is bad or when they are over. Camellias are less demanding than rhododendrons; they will grow in sun, providing the soil is moist and summer conditions are not baking hot, and also tolerate neutral, but not chalky soil. No regular pruning is needed; just tidy the shape. Rejuvenate old, leggy or badly out-of-shape camellias by cutting back into old thick wood - or even just a stump - in spring, though expect it to take a few years to start flowering again.

C. j. 'R.L. Wheeler'

C. j. 'Desire'

C. *x* williamsii 'Cherub'

C. j. 'Devonia'

C. j. 'Raspberry Ripple'

C. j. 'Ballet Dancer'

C. j. 'Bill Stewart'

C. j. 'Konronkoku' ('Nigra')

Left: *As the flowers start dying, gently nip off the dead heads between thumb and fingernail. This improves the shrub's appearance and allows new shoots to emerge from behind the old flowers. Avoid damaging new shoots when deadheading.*

C. j. 'Candidissima'

C. j. 'Reg Ragland'

C. j. 'Furo-an'

C. j. 'Blaze of Glory'

C. j. 'Tinker Bell'

C. j. 'Guiseppina Pierri'

Pruning a camellia in a pot

Improve lopsided camellias by pruning them hard immediately after the flowers are finished. You can do this to plants growing in the garden or new plants still in their pots. Cut back all shoots growing over to one side.

1 *Cut back to a short shoot close to the base of the plant to encourage new growth.*

2 *If there are no suitably placed shoots, cut just above a leaf joint instead.*

3 *Pinch out the growing tips of new shoots when they are about 3in(7.5cm) long to encourage further branching.*

Right: *Try to choose a camellia that is a compact shape, branching and fairly symmetrical like the one on the left. In time, a lopsided plant with few sideshoots can be improved by pruning. Weeds or liverwort in the pot suggest that the plant needs feeding.*

Chaenomeles

Chaenomeles japonica is an old cottage garden favorite, commonly called ornamental quince (and sometimes confused with the true edible quince, which is larger). It is a medium-sized shrub with roughly golf ball-sized fruits that ripen to a golden yellow and hang on the plant well into winter. The early spring flowers are stunning; chalice shaped, with a pool of golden stamens in the center, growing in clusters against the twiggy outline of the shrub and timed to coincide with the arrival of the first few leaves, which give them a natural background. There is a good range of cultivars, with flowers in white, red, pink and salmon shades. *Chaenomeles* is a very easy plant to accommodate, thriving in virtually any garden soil, in sun or light shade. It is usually grown as a free-standing shrub, but is seen at its most spectacular trained out against a wall. Either way, it needs little pruning; with older plants, remove a few of the oldest branches as low down as possible each year, just after flowering. Remove congested branches or those growing strongly out from the wall.

1 *If your only option is a rather shapeless plant, prune it before planting in spring or early summer. This will improve the shape and create a good framework for the future. If you plant in late summer, fall or winter, do not prune until spring.*

2 *Cut back all the long shoots that spoil the shape of the plant, cutting just above a leaf joint or young shoot about 6-8in (15-20cm) from the top of the pot.*

GOOD PLANT
This Chaenomeles x superba 'Geisha Girl' *is compact and branching freely from the base. With a plant in flower, you can see that it matches the label.*

BAD PLANT
A long, leggy plant will branch, if at all, from the ends of the shoots, giving a rather open, untidy sort of bush.

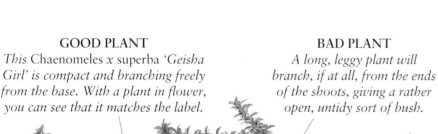

3 *Aim for a good, well-shaped, branching framework of short stems in the base of the plant. Over the following growing season, plenty of new shoots will develop, resulting in a dense, twiggy plant with plenty of flowers.*

Left: *Chaenomeles are very versatile; they can be grown as shrubs or trained against a wall, either allowed to grow naturally or trained into formal fan or espalier shapes. Here, a lovely C. speciosa 'Moerloosei' has been informally trained onto a wall.*

Chaenomeles against a wall

To train a chaenomeles against a wall, spread out the main stems and tie them to horizontal wires secured to wall nails. Wall-trained chaenomeles need regular tying in to keep them growing flat against their support. This will encourage sideshoots that, with luck, will grow flush with the wall and can be trained in. Horizontal branches flower much better than upright ones.

Below: *Immediately after flowering, shorten outward-growing shoots back to a few inches from the wall. Make sure your secateurs are sharp.*

Above: *Tie in any shoots growing out over the wall. They will increase the branch structure and create extra flowering space.*

Above: *Chaenomeles produces suckers from the base. Remove these from a wall-trained shrub because they spoil the shape.*

Chaenomeles is also known as flowering quince. The fruits, though not edible, are quite harmless.

4 *The finished result may look about half the size of the shrub you bought, but it will make a plant at least twice as good. It will soon replace the lost growth.*

Right: *Chaenomeles also suit a huge range of planting schemes. They are traditionally grown in cottage gardens, but when allowed to grow unpruned, make charming, natural-looking shrubs for a wild garden. This is C. speciosa 'Knap Hill Scarlet'.*

Choisya

Evergreen shrubs form the basic framework of the garden. They provide year-round interest and, strategically placed, can form an invaluable screen. But some evergreens grown primarily for their foliage can look distinctly uninteresting and, if overdone, result in a garden that does not appear to change from one season to the next. This is where *Choisya ternata* wins hands down. Its clusters of good-sized, pretty, single white flowers cover the bushes in late spring or early summer, with occasional blooms later in summer, and a second, smaller, flush in early fall after a good summer. As an extra bonus, both the flowers and foliage are scented. The blossom is perfumed like orange blossom, hence the plant's common name, Mexican orange blossom. The foliage releases aromatic oils every time it is touched, so plant *Choisya* at the side of a path or by a doorway. It is an undemanding shrub to grow, tolerating most reasonable soils and sun or light shade.

The tips of the shoots may suffer slight dieback after severe frosts - the golden form 'Sundance' is specially prone to this - so in cold climates grow *Choisya* in a sheltered situation or, ideally, against a sunny wall. Keep large old plants in trim by cutting out a few of the oldest shoots each year after flowering; this encourages new growth to shoot from the base of the plant, producing a more compact shape.

Left: A single Choisya *plant is enough to perfume quite a large area. For maximum perfume-power, grow the plant in a sheltered spot where the scent won't be dispersed by the breeze.*

Right: The gold-leaved form of Choisya ternata, *called 'Sundance', makes a bright splash of color in a sunny mixed border. In shade, the color is more lime green than gold.*

Frost damage

Choisyas can suffer from frost damage in cold areas; normally only the tips of some shoots are affected. Simply prune these back to good healthy growth in late spring, after the risk of further hard frost is past. If you grow a specimen in a container, move the plant to a more protected spot, such as under a car port or even into a cold greenhouse during severe conditions.

Above: 'Aztec Pearl' is grown for its specially prolific flowers. It makes a neat bush with more elegant foliage than C. ternata, *which gives it a rather lighter effect when not in flower.*

Choisya in tubs

Plant Choisya in a soil-based potting mixture. As it grows, prune the shoot tips as necessary to maintain a domed shape. Feed and water regularly during the summer and prevent waterlogging in winter by raising the tub up on bricks.

Right: Being naturally small and compact, C. ternata 'Sundance' makes a good shrub for growing in tubs. Expect a light crop of flowers in early summer. Protect the plant from frost in winter.

Left: The flowers of C. arizonica 'Aztec Pearl' are bigger and produced in larger clusters - more like apple blossom - than those of Choisya ternata. Their scent is less pronounced, and the leaves are narrow and elongated in shape.

Cistus

Cistus is a striking and useful mini-shrub for the front of a sunny border, on a rock garden, or for a low informal edging to a path. The flowers - in white, plus pink and mauve shades - look like large poppies up to about 3in(7.5cm) across, complete with artistically crumpled petals, though they are less fragile than they look. Flowering continues for almost three months in midsummer. The plant tolerates almost any amount of heat, though it is only about as hardy as *Hebe* and dislikes very cold winters. Fortunately, cuttings root easily, so if climate is a problem, simply keep a few 'spares' in pots on the windowsill through the winter. Cistus are natural sunlovers, whose main requirements are sun, shelter and very well-drained soil - wet winters spell an early death. As the plants survive drought so well, they are a good choice for potential problem areas, such as hot dry banks, raised beds, hollow-topped walls and patio planters. They associate well with other heat and sunlovers, including hebes, lavenders and phlomis, silver-foliage plants, such as *Artemisia*, and mulleins, such as *Verbascum bombyciferum*, and smaller flowers that enjoy the same conditions, including helianthemums, pinks and diascia. Use cistus for adding seasonal highlights to groups of all-year-round evergreens. The plants are so easy to propagate that once a few favorite varieties are in the garden, they can be duplicated endlessly to provide carpets of color in any situation with suitable soil.

Right: Cistus x cyprius *is one of the larger members of the cistus family. It grows to nearly 6ft(1.8m) high and has flowers measuring 3in(7.5cm) in diameter. It makes a good flowering hedge for an exposed coastal situation in full sun and dry soil.*

Choosing a good plant

BAD PLANT
Avoid a tall, sparse and spindly plant. Dead leaves and shoots, plus lengths of bare stem are signs of neglect.

GOOD PLANT
Choose a compact, bushy plant with plenty of healthy green foliage and no brown tips or dead shoots.

Above and right: *Improve a poor plant by cutting back dead twigs to their junction with green tissue. Shorten long shoots to just above a strong pair of leaves.*

Below: Cistus *x* purpureus *is a useful shrub for a bank or sunny well-drained border. It grows to 3ft(90cm) high and roughly the same spread. The chocolate central blotches are a feature of this hybrid.*

Propagation

Cistus roots easily from cuttings. Snip off 2-3in(5-7.5cm)-long tips of young shoots in midsummer, remove the lower leaves, cut through the stem cleanly with a sharp knife just below a leaf joint and dip into rooting hormone powder. Fill a 3.5in(9cm) pot with seed mixture and push five cuttings in round the edge of the pot to about halfway. Slip the pot inside a loose plastic bag and keep it out of direct sun until the cuttings have rooted - probably six to eight weeks later. Always take more cuttings than you need and choose the strongest ones to pot up singly. Plant them out when the new pot is full of roots.

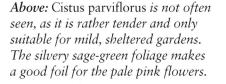

Above: Cistus parviflorus *is not often seen, as it is rather tender and only suitable for mild, sheltered gardens. The silvery sage-green foliage makes a good foil for the pale pink flowers.*

Above: Cistus pulverulentus *has narrower foliage and almost magenta-colored flowers. It is a naturally dwarf variety, suitable for a rock garden or at the front of a well-drained border.*

Cytisus and Genista

Broom is the common name shared by two very similar genera of shrubs: *Cytisus* and *Genista*. Both have pealike flowers and wiry stems, bearing leaves so tiny that at first glance they do not appear to exist. *Cytisus* brooms include many hybrids that generally make rather open, stemmy, medium-sized shrubs. The flowers, which appear from early to midsummer, may be yellow, white, pink, mauve, red or purple, though some have very attractive two-tone blooms. The *Genista* brooms are less commonly seen; they are mainly compact, low-growing, mound-forming plants, with yellow flowers in early summer, though one of the most attractive is actually a small tree - the Mount Etna Broom *(Genista aetnensis)*. All the brooms need similar conditions: a sunny situation and well-drained soil. Poor soils are a positive advantage, as brooms flower better when half-starved; in rich soil, flowering is poor. Windy sites are not a problem either, as the virtually leafless stems are specially adapted for life in exposed windy situations. Bigger brooms, such as *Cytisus,* are useful for hot dry borders, while the smaller genistas are at home on rockeries and dry banks or overhanging low walls or steps. Once established, they need virtually no attention. Pruning can prove fatal and feeding is unnecessary. However, brooms are not very long-lived; ten years represents a good life, after which plants need replacing. Plants seed themselves freely, although seedlings are 'mongrels' and not usually identical to the parents.

Left: C. 'Zeelandia' is a popular hybrid with tricolor flowers of cream, pink and mauve in late spring and early summer. This and the other hybrids prefer better soil than the species.

Below: Genista aetnensis *flowers in early summer and reaches about 12ft (3.7m) in height and spread. It prefers an acid or neutral soil, but tolerates chalk as long as the soil is otherwise good.*

Left: Cytisus purpureus, *the purple broom, is a good compact species for a rock garden or a windy spot with poor soil - an ideal candidate for covering a difficult exposed bank in full sun.*

Choosing a broom

Cytisus scoparius 'Firefly' *(below left) is a traditional broom that makes a loose, open, bushy shape up to 4ft(1.2m) high and wide, with flowers in early summer. Genista lydia (right), a low, dome-shaped dwarf shrub, is ideal for an exposed situation, a rockery or over the edge of a wall; it flowers in late spring.*

Below: The pineapple-scented flowers of C. battandieri *appear in early mid-summer and the silky foliage is a good feature. Train it on a sunny wall.*

Above: Brooms can be used in adventurous plant associations. Here a white-flowered cytisus is growing in a dry garden alongside senecio, ornamental grasses and valerian.

Escallonia

You do not often find an evergreen shrub that puts on a good show of flower *and* has a long flowering season, but this is what makes escallonia special. The individual flowers are not particularly big, but grow in small clusters, smothering the plants from early summer until the fall. *Escallonia* is very tolerant of poor growing conditions; it puts up with polluted air, sea breezes, dry or chalky soil, even clay, but it must have sun for at least half the day. It is not the most hardy of shrubs, however, which is why it is common in coastal regions where hard frosts are scarce. In a cold region, train it against a sunny wall. All escallonias have pink, red or white flowers. Choose *E. macrantha* for a flowering hedge close to the coast. It has deep pink flowers and a tough disposition and makes a thick hedge up to 8ft(2.5m) high. For general garden use, cultivars such as 'Donard Seedling' and 'Apple Blossom' are popular and make compact, slow-growing, medium to large specimens. Since escallonia naturally makes tight dense growth, pruning is not really essential. Plants grown as informal hedges can often be left for several years without any trimming or reshaping. If grown as a formal hedge, give it an annual trim in early fall after the last flowers are over. When grown as a shrub, either trim it into semi-formal shapes or leave the plants to assume a natural bushy shape. Any straggly or out-of-place branches can be tidied after flowering.

General care

No regular pruning is needed, but remove dead shoots and old flower spikes to keep the shrubs tidy. If plants need reshaping, cut out old flowered stems as soon as the flowers are over. Cut old, neglected plants back hard once in late spring to rejuvenate them.

Right: The graceful arching habit and strong color of 'Donard Brilliance' are unusual among escallonias. Grow it as a specimen shrub or in a large border. This variety may be hard to find.

Below: E. rubra 'Woodside' is an unusually small, compact cultivar. Its small size and neat shape make it ideal for a rock garden, raised bed or bank - in fact, anywhere with good drainage.

Below: 'Apple Blossom' is one of the best-known escallonia cultivars, slow-growing, with striking flowers of pink and white. Like most escallonias, it continues to flower from midsummer right through into late fall.

Right: Their long flowering season makes escallonias specially valuable evergreen shrubs for mixed borders. The small foliage is a useful foil to bulbs and early bedding at the start of the season. This is 'Apple Blossom'.

Choosing a good escallonia

Poor plants have long bare stems with new growth only apparent towards the tips. Such plants have probably sat around in the same container at the nursery for some time and become 'starved' of feed. The foliage may also look pale or yellowish. A good plant should be dense and bushy, with a roughly symmetrical shape. The one pictured far right has the potential to flower well right from the start, and will need just light shaping to develop into an attractive shrub.

BAD PLANT
Avoid long, leafless stems.

GOOD PLANT
Choose a bushy, well-shaped plant.

Forsythia

One of the unofficial signs that spring is well under way is the appearance of forsythia in gardens. The wandlike shoots, loaded with masses of star-shaped yellow flowers, are immediately recognizable. At first glance it may seem as if there is only one kind of forsythia, but by examining several plants flowering side by side in a nursery, small variations between flower shapes and shades become apparent from one cultivar to the next. Arguably the best is 'Lynwood', which has deep egg-yolk yellow flowers and the broadest petals. This and the other common varieties, 'Beatrix Farrand' and the narrow-petalled 'Spectabilis', all make large, rather straggly shrubs up to 8ft(2.5m) high and 6ft(1.8m) or more across, so allow them plenty of space as they do not like heavy pruning. Where space is really restricted, there is a dwarf forsythia, *F. viridissima* 'Bronxensis', that grows barely more than 18x18in(45x45cm) - ideal for a raised bed or rock garden. Forsythia is justifiably popular for its reliable, free-flowering habit and easy, grow-anywhere temperament. It does best in sun, although some slight shade is acceptable. There is nothing you can do to alter the naturally open, untidy shape of forsythia, but cut back the flowering stems when the flowers are over, and once the plant is more than five years old it is a good idea to shorten any long branches that otherwise spoil the shrub's shape. This, too, is best done just after flowering. Although forsythia is normally grown as a shrub in a border, one of the most attractive ways of using it is as an informal flowering hedge. By trimming it lightly back into shape with shears when the flowers go over, you automatically prune the plants correctly to encourage a good flowering habit and maintain the shape of the hedge. The dense twiggy interior is a great favorite with nesting birds!

Above: *Even a young forsythia plant straight from the nursery will carry flowers. Choose a bushy plant with a symmetrical shape and plenty of healthy new growth. Avoid leggy plants with masses of bare stems or dead leaves.*

Left: *Forsythia is one of the most prolific spring shrubs; every branch of a well-grown specimen has the potential to be covered with dazzling yellow flowers from top to bottom. This is* Forsythia x intermedia *'Spectabilis'.*

Pruning forsythia

Free-standing shrubs should be pruned after flowering. Remove the ends of stems that carried the current year's flowers (you should be able to see the remains of the dead flowers or the stalks they grew from) and cut back to just above an unflowered sideshoot. This not only tidies the shape of the shrub, but also stops it outgrowing its space.

Above: A forsythia hedge can look stunning in spring when it is in full flower. This one has been cut into an informal billowing shape and makes an effective screen. Avoid clipping parts of a hedge that you suspect may be a bird's nesting site until after the young ones have flown.

A forsythia hedge

Forsythia makes a wonderful flowering hedge. Instead of trimming it in a straight line, why not experiment with a castellated top for added interest? Clip back the hedge after flowering to remove as many of the old flowered stems as possible. Do not be tempted to 'tidy' it again later or you risk losing some of the following year's flowers.

Hamamelis

Witch hazels may not have the biggest, showiest or most colorful flowers in the garden, but they are among the most highly rated, as they open when hardly anything else is in flower. Given a mild fall, the first spidery blooms start appearing on the bare stems almost as soon as the leaves have dropped and continue right through until early spring. If the weather is too cold, blooming will be delayed till spring when conditions are better. Although individual flowers are thin-petaled, they grow in fair-sized clusters that show up well, particularly against a suitable background. The trick of growing witch hazels lies very much in choosing the right situation. They need reasonably well-drained soil that is low in lime (acid to neutral is best). People are often tempted to grow them in much wetter conditions than they like. They also need sun and shelter to ripen the wood for a good flowering display. Plant them against a backdrop of dark green and gold-variegated evergreens or different colored conifers to help show the flowers up and create a coordinated winter display. Given the right spot, witch hazels grow happily and need little attention apart from routine damage repairs.

Below: Witch hazels show up best against a dark background that contrasts with their flowers. Make even more of a show by adding a carpet of complementary flowers, such as these 'Springwood White' heathers.

Hamamelis *x* intermedia
'Primavera'

Hamamelis *x* intermedia
'Pallida'

Hamamelis *x* intermedia
'Diane'

Hamamelis *x* intermedia
'Carmine Red'

Above: *Site red-flowered varieties, such as this 'Ruby Glow', with care. Though bright, they can literally vanish into a winter landscape. Plain evergreens make an ideal background.*

Dealing with suckers on hamamelis

Hamamelis may produce strong suckers, particularly if the plant has been moved or the roots or base of the stem damaged, encouraging adventitious buds to develop and grow into shoots. Deal with suckers in spring, as it is easy to tell from the flowers which are the shoots of your named variety and which the rogues. If you leave the job till later, mark the stems to be taken out with colored string to avoid mistakes. Expect some new shoots to appear from low down in what is left of the plant after dealing with suckers; some will be the named variety and some will be more suckers. As a general rule, you can tell them apart as suckers arise from below ground and stems of the named variety from the main stems above ground.

1 *Hamamelis that produce two types of flowers on the same plant or a profusion of non-flowering twigs (as here), are usually found to have developed suckers from the rootstock.*

2 *Trace the non-flowering shoots or those with the wrong color flowers back to ground level and cut them out. If left, they would take over from the named variety.*

Left: *Hamamelis also have brilliant tints in the fall. Red-flowered cultivars, such as this 'Diane', generally have red-tinted leaves, while yellow-flowered kinds have gold tints.*

Right: *Seen at close quarters, the intricate feathery structure of the witch hazel flower looks too fragile to survive cold winter weather, but it is surprisingly durable and even delicately scented.*

Hebe

Hebes, once called veronica, are small, bushy, summer-flowering evergreen shrubs with characteristic bottlebrush-like flowers, mainly in shades of pink, purple and mauve. They are very good value in a small garden, where they occupy little space and provide a flowering display from early to late summer. A sunny, sheltered spot in light, free-draining soil is essential, as hebes are not reliably hardy in colder climates. The problem of cold winters can be overcome to some extent by growing them close to the house, in front of a sunny wall or in pots on the patio. During prolonged cold spells in winter, lag free-standing plants with horticultural fleece, old net curtains or sheets of newspaper. Protect potgrown plants by moving them into a cold greenhouse, unheated porch or sunroom until spring. In cold regions, it is also worth rooting a few cuttings in late summer and keeping them in pots on a windowsill indoors for the winter. Variegated hebes make very attractive plants for winter or even all-year-round decoration in a cold conservatory or cool sunroom; they will flower for much longer indoors than out, provided they receive enough light. Hebes with 'whipcord' foliage are grown mainly for their khaki or green scaly stems - the flowers are generally insignificant.

Hebe corstorphinensis
'Cranleighensis'

Hebe formosa x franciscana
'Variegata'

Hebe gracillima
'Great Orme'

Hebe matthewsii
'Midsummer Beauty'

Hebe amplexicaulis
'Amy'

Taking cuttings

1 *In midsummer, snip off healthy, non-flowering 2-3in(5-7.5cm)-long shoots and strip away the leaves from the bottom half of each stem, taking care not to 'peel' the stems.*

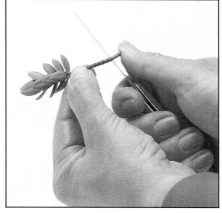

2 *Cut the base of the cutting cleanly just below a leaf joint; you can see where the leaves were attached to the stem. Rooting powder is not essential, but dip the cut ends into it if available.*

3 *Fill a pot with seed mix and gently push each cutting in as far as the bottom leaves. Firm the mix lightly with your fingertips, then water well to settle the mix around the cuttings.*

Cutting out brown stems

Old hebe plants sometimes splay apart or develop brown shoots, especially after a cold winter. Tidy them up in mid- to late spring. Gently pulling the branches apart often reveals plenty of new young growth. Prune back damaged stems, cutting as low down in the plant as possible, to allow the new growth to take over.

1 *Prune damaged or browning hebe stems back to a junction with a green, healthy looking stem or close to ground level.*

2 *Young shoots growing right down in the center of the plant will quickly develop and fill in the bare patches left after pruning.*

4 *A plastic bag placed loosely over the pot creates humid air that stops the cuttings drying out. A short stick in the middle of the pot holds the plastic off the foliage if the bag sags.*

Pruning hebe

You can even rejuvenate elderly, balding and overgrown hebes by cutting back the old branches in mid-spring, once you are sure that there are a few new young shoots forming in the base of the plant to replace them. If not, just cut back about one third of the old stems; this will encourage young growth to develop from the center of the plant. Remove a few more older stems each spring.

Hebe *x* andersonii 'Variegata'

Hebe 'Louise'

Above: *Hebes are dwarf evergreen shrubs that mostly originate from New Zealand. Although they need a sheltered site inland, on the coast they tolerate surprisingly windy conditions without coming to any harm.*

Helianthemum

Not all shrubs can be measured in feet; some, such as *Helianthemum*, would barely make the grade. Despite its woody stems, which persist throughout winter (technically confirming it as a shrub), *Helianthemum* is, in fact, often listed in catalogs with the perennial flowers. These small, neat, bushy, mound-shaped plants are most at home in the well-drained, sunny conditions of a rock garden, although they also thrive on sunny banks or towards the front of a well-drained border where the soil is not particularly rich. (Clay soils, shade, and winter wet are the kiss of death.) Helianthemums flower from late spring to midsummer, with brightly colored, fragile blooms that look very much like wide open poppies but less than half the size. Depending on cultivar, these may be pink, orange, red or white, each with a small, fluffy yellow boss in the center. Take advantage of its dense ground-hugging habit to use helianthemum as ground cover for a hot, sunny, dry bank, or team it with other plants that enjoy the same conditions, such as pinks, hebes, ornamental sages and cistus. Helianthemums are very easy to care for; they can largely be left to their own devices. Deadheading keeps the plants looking tidy when the flowers are over, but this is a tedious job as there are so many blooms - the plants do not suffer if you overlook it. But do cut back straggling, untidy stems then, to preserve the shape of the plants. As helianthemums strike very easily from cuttings, you can make use of the new shoots that grow up in summer after flowering has finished. Root them in pots of seed mixture in a cool, slightly shady spot.

Below: H. 'Rhodanthe Carneum' has silvery-gray foliage with a slightly felty texture that sets off the fragile-looking pastel petals particularly well.

Above: The glossy white foliage and brilliant white poppylike flowers of H. serpyllifolium 'The Bride' stand out well in a rock garden or at the front of a dry border. Plants are almost hidden by bloom in midsummer.

Right: At the nursery, helianthemums may look a little open and floppy; once planted, they soon fill out to make low, dense clumps. Choose a plant with plenty of shoots from the base.

Left: *The wild rock rose,* H. nummularium, *native to Britain and Europe, is the 'parent' of most of the variously colored hybrids grown in gardens today. It is an exceptionally rugged plant that grows naturally in rock crevices.*

Below: *The very bright red of* H. *'Fire Dragon' contrasts well with deep greens. For maximum impact, team it with contrasting foliage shapes, such as that of the bearded iris plant seen here.*

Above: *Try growing helianthemums in a bed with similarly circular flowers such as violas, but in contrasting colors. Mauve and purple shades look good with them, and helianthemums do not appear in those colors.*

Hibiscus

Hardy hibiscus *(Hibiscus syriacus)* is perfect for adding a taste of the tropics to a garden in a cool climate. Its large, showy, colorful flowers up to 3in(7.5cm) across, with their prominent stamens, look a touch tougher than those of the popular tropical houseplant to which it is related. Hardy hibiscus does not flower until late summer, but then keeps going almost up to the frost. This makes it specially valuable in a border, as it starts to bloom just as most summer flowers are coming to an end. The best known color is blue, but there are also pinky-mauve and white cultivars, often with a contrasting bright spot of color inside the throat. The plant is easy to accommodate as it naturally makes a neat upright shape that needs no pruning, and being slow and stocky, it never outgrows its welcome. Team it with late-flowering plants that enjoy similar conditions, such as hebes, penstemons and silver foliage artemisias, or grow it as a specimen plant by the door. Hardy hibiscus thrives in a warm, sunny spot with well-drained soil and must have shelter from wind damage, which causes the buds and large flowers to turn brown, especially white blooms. The rare and fragile double-flowered hibiscuses are particularly prone to this and are best grown in large pots in a sunroom or conservatory, though they could stand outdoors on a sheltered patio in summer.

Above: The best single blue cultivar is H. syriacus *'Blue Bird'*. Its large flowers are prolific, rain-proof, fade-resistant and long-lasting, and make this probably the most popular hardy hibiscus of them all. It is also known by its French name, 'Oiseau Bleu'.

Left: In the garden, the purple-eyed, mauvey-blue flowers of H. syriacus *'Blue Bird'* add an exotic touch to more commonplace plants. The shrubs can be grown on their own as specimen plants or with others in borders. They naturally make a neat, compact shape without trimming.

Above: 'Woodbridge' has single mauve-pink flowers with a mauve eye. Grow it with 'Blue Bird' and exotic foliage plants for a subtropical look.

Left: Hibiscus 'Red Heart' is less often seen. Unlike many large white shrub flowers, these do not turn brown when the blooms go over. It looks superb in a tub with variegated abutilon.

Above: This is the superb Hibiscus 'Woodbridge'. Hardy hibiscus flowers are just as large, showy and colorful as those of their indoor cousin and the only choice for growing outdoors, except in a near tropical climate.

45

Hydrangea

Hydrangeas are much more versatile than they are usually given credit for. They are among the few plants with large colorful blooms that will flower well in shade, they enjoy wet conditions and tolerate a wide range of soils, from fairly acid to moderately alkaline. The best-known hydrangeas are the Hortensia group, with the familiar dense, domed heads of flower, usually in pink or blue. Lacecaps are very similar, but the central florets are sterile, making it look as though the flowers in the center of each group have not opened. The climbing hydrangea, *H. petiolaris*, is good for a shady wall. It has white flowers, but is notoriously slow to start producing them. Species hydrangeas are less familiar, but very striking plants. *H. aspera* Villosa Group has lavender lacecap flowers and tolerates chalky soil; the giant *H. sargentiana* has shaggy bark, large, rough-textured, evergreen leaves and large pale lilac-blue mophead flowers, but must have acid soil. All hydrangeas thrive in woodland gardens, as long as the soil is sufficiently moist. In a more conventional garden, grow them in shade under trees, among larger shrubs in borders, or to brighten up shady corners.

Changing the color

1 *Grow pink varieties of hortensia hydrangeas on chalky soil to keep them pink and blue ones on acid soil to keep them blue. If you grow blue types on chalky soil, use a hydrangea colorant or they will turn pink.*

2 *Mix the product (which is based on aluminum sulfate) with water and apply it to the plants following the maker's directions; repeat the treatment regularly during the growing season for maximum effect.*

Taking cuttings

Hydrangeas are very easy to propagate from cuttings. In midsummer, snip off the tip of a young shoot with about three pairs of leaves. Always choose perfect, healthy shoots for propagation purposes.

1 *Cut off the bottom leaves flush with the stem, taking care not to 'peel' the skin, otherwise the cutting may rot.*

2 *Nip out the tiny underdeveloped leaves enclosing the bud at the top of the shoot between your fingernails. Leave just one healthy pair of leaves at the very top of the stem.*

3 *With a sharp knife, trim the base of the cutting, making a straight cut immediately below the bottom pair of leaf scars. Be very careful when using a knife in this way.*

4 *Dip the stem in rooting hormone, which helps prevent rotting. Push cuttings into seed mix, to about 0.5in (1.25cm) below the leaves.*

Pruning

Hydrangeas need little pruning. Deadhead young plants in early spring after the frosts. Cut out a few of the oldest stems of old plants at ground level.

1 This stem has been killed by late frost. Prune back in spring, cutting just above a plump healthy bud.

2 If only the tip of the shoot is damaged, cut just below a fat green bud. The remaining buds will develop and shoots that grow from them will carry the following year's flowers.

3 Soil that is roughly neutral can be altered to suit various hydrangeas more easily - use lime to make the soil more alkaline or, as here, add a quantity of peat to make it more acid.

H. aspera Villosa Group reaches 10ft(3m) high and wide; it has dark, felty foliage and pale purple lacecap-type flowers in late summer.

H. arborescens 'Annabelle' flowers from midsummer into early fall.

H. arborescens 'Annabelle' makes a dome-shaped shrub about 3-4ft(90-120cm) high.

H. paniculata 'Grandiflora' makes a 6ft(1.8m) shrub that flowers in late summer and early fall. The white flower heads slowly fade to pale pink.

Above: Leave dead flower heads on throughout the winter, as they protect the dormant buds lower down from frost. In spring, cut them off just above a cluster of healthy leaves.

Hypericum

Hypericums are indestructible plants that are useful for a wide range of 'difficult' situations. Toughest of the lot is *Hypericum calycinum*, which has large, chalice-shaped, golden flowers with huge central bosses of feathery stamens from mid- to late summer. This is the one to choose for dry soil under trees or in searing sun, and also borders in family gardens that are likely to be the target of stray footballs and boisterous dogs. On steep banks that are difficult to mow, a dense ground cover of hypericum makes a good substitute for grass; it smothers out weeds and never needs cutting. Given good growing conditions, however, it can be rather invasive, so keep it for 'problem' areas - any other than wet. More sophisticated are the slightly taller *H.* x *moserianum* 'Tricolor' (with narrow, pink-cream-and-green variegated leaves), and 'Elstead, which has red, upright capsicum-like fruits; the two make a good team in well- drained sunny areas. The very popular *Hypericum* 'Hidcote' makes a spreading bushy shrub that is taller still; it is another good candidate for fending off hard wear in family gardens, and has an even longer flowering season than *calycinum*. All the hypericums are very easy to grow; they do best in poor, dry soils and need little attention beyond an annual cutting back in spring. Low kinds are cut back almost to ground level, while taller kinds are merely topped. This encourages fresh new growth and avoids a build-up of old, non-flowering shoots in the bush and the risk of harboring rust. Failure to prune is responsible for old hypericum plants looking neglected and unattractive, and is one of the main reasons for the plants' poor reputation in some quarters.

H. androsaemum *'Orange Flair'* produces yellow flowers in summer, followed by masses of long-lasting, bright orange-red berries, which remain on the plants well into fall and winter. Grows to 3-4ft (90-120cm).

H. erectum *'Gemo' is* a new introduction with slender foliage on upright stems and masses of small, fluffy-centered yellow flowers from early to late summer. Grows to 3-4ft (90-120cm).

Left: Hypericum calycinum *(rose of Sharon) makes good evergreen ground cover for banks and other dry places in sun or light shade, but can become a bit rampant in better growing conditions.*

Right: H. 'Hidcote' *makes a mound-shaped plant up to 6ft(1.8m) high. This good border plant is studded with golden flowers from mid-summer until fall. It is a highly popular garden shrub.*

H. x moserianum 'Tricolor' *is an old favorite, a dwarf shrub with pretty tricolored foliage. The single yellow flowers are produced in summer and fall. It grows 24in(60cm) high and wide, but is less robust than most hypericums, so provide a more sheltered spot.*

Taking cuttings

2 *Remove the soft growing tip and any immature leaves from the top of the cutting. Leave no soft or damaged material that might rot.*

1 *Snip 6in(15cm)-long tips from young shoots in midsummer. Keeping them the right way up, remove all but the top pair of leaves.*

3 *Trim the base below the point where the lowest leaves were attached. Use a sharp knife and cut on a wooden board to be safe.*

4 *Dip the cut end into rooting hormone powder if you wish and insert three cuttings around the edge of a pot filled with seed mix.*

5 *Water well and cover with a plastic bag. After 6-8 weeks, pot plants individually and grow on till big enough to plant in the garden.*

Lavandula

Lavender is something of a dual-purpose plant - part herb and part small shrub. The flowers can be dried and tied into bunches to perfume drawers, or separated and used in potpourri - even added to mixed Mediterranean herbs and used in cookery. Although lavender flowers are best known for their perfume, in fact the leaves are also scented, so it pays to grow the plant where people will brush against it, if you want to make the most of this feature. Being evergreen, the scent of the foliage, though weaker than that of the flowers, is present all year round. Lavender likes a typical herb situation - warm, sheltered and sunny, with not too rich but well-drained soil. Avoid winter wet at all costs. Plants can be grown in a mixed border with other flowers and shrubs that enjoy the same sort of growing conditions, but a row of identical plants makes a good, low, flowering hedge or edging to a path or formal bed. Compact varieties can also be grown in terracotta pots on a patio or path close to the house. Various lavenders are available, from tall shrubby kinds with long-stemmed flowers (English lavenders, the best for perfume) to neater, more compact kinds (best for low hedges). French lavenders have a pair of long petals like flags flying from the tip of each flower head (these are the most decorative, and best for cooking), and there is even a rare green lavender that is quite tricky to grow. All lavenders are summer-flowering and attract huge numbers of bees and other insects. If allergy to bee stings is a problem, plant lavenders well away from paths and children's play areas.

Right: As a change, there are a very few pink-flowered cultivars. This is Lavandula angustifolia 'Hidcote Pink', one of the best pink types.

Deadheading

Once lavender flowers start to fade, go over the plants with secateurs or shears and trim off the old heads, also removing the tips of the young leafy shoots below them. This keeps the plant tidy and regularly rejuvenated. Never cut back into old brown wood or you could kill the plant.

Taking cuttings

1 *Young plants make the best 'parents'. In mid-summer, take 3in (7.5cm) lengths from the tips of young, pale green, pliable, non-flowering shoots.*

2 *Carefully remove the leaves from the bottom one third to one half of each cutting, taking care not to 'peel' the stems. Prepare a pot with seed mix.*

3 Dip the cut ends into rooting powder. Tap gently to remove surplus. Push the cuttings into seed mix and firm around them. If the stems are soft, make a hole first.

4 Space the cuttings about 1in(2.5cm) apart. When the pot is full of cuttings, water them and cover the pot with a plastic bag. This traps humid air around the shoots so that they do not dry out.

Below: French lavender (Lavandula stoechas) has strongly colored flowers and aromatic foliage. This plant is L.s. pendunculata.

A lavender hedge

L. angustifolia 'Munstead' has a naturally compact habit, which makes it the best variety for dwarf hedging.

1 When young plants fill their pots, cut back the tops to tidy them and encourage bushy growth. By this time, the young plants will be ready for planting.

2 To make a dwarf hedge, plant a straight row of lavenders about 6in(15cm) apart in a warm sheltered spot. Plant into well-prepared soil, without breaking up the rootballs.

3 Water in new plants and continue watering when the soil is dry for the first few months until the plants are established.

Right: A dwarf hedge of lavender makes a neat path edging and is ideal for outlining a formal feature such as a herb garden. This deep purple-flowered cultivar is 'Hidcote'. Clip plants after flowering to keep them in shape.

Lavatera

Tree mallows are one of the 'must-have' garden fashion accessories of the decade. Although they are woody stemmed plants and as such usually treated like shrubs, they actually behave more like herbaceous flowers in most gardens and die back to ground level in winter. It is best to leave old stems on the plants during winter to help protect the crowns - covering them with a few inches of strawy organic matter as for hardy fuchsias is also helpful. With their clusters of hollyhock-like stems and flowers, tree mallows are good for growing among herbaceous flowers and roses in a cottage-style garden, or among other flowering shrubs in a more modern style design. Plants are fast growing and quick to establish, but need well-drained soil and sunny sheltered conditions to thrive. They tolerate seaside conditions happily.

Propagating tree mallows

Tree mallows are comparatively shortlived, so it is a good idea to propagate new plants occasionally. Some of the species, such as Lavatera olbia 'Rosea', can be easily raised from seed (but check the packet or seed catalog before buying, as many lavateras are only annuals or biennials). Plants can also be raised from cuttings, which root very easily. This is the only way of being sure that named cultivars, such as the popular red-eyed pale pink Lavatera assurgentiflora 'Barnsley', remain true to type. In areas with cold winters, insure against winter losses by taking cuttings of the young shoots that grow from the base of the plant in summer. Root them in small pots of seed mixture, and keep them under cover for the winter.

Below: *'Bredon Springs' is a beautiful deep pink. Sedum spectabile, hebes and perennial herbs look good with lavatera and enjoy similar conditions.*

Above: *In a sheltered spot, tree mallow makes an informal flowering hedge that can either stand alone or provide a colorful background.*

Left: In a herbaceous border, Lavatera assurgentiflora 'Barnsley' provides a useful variation in height and habit. For maximum impact, blend flowers with strong shapes, such as upright spikes, flat umbels, and frothy bunches.

Below: When grown as a specimen plant in a sunny spot and correctly pruned each spring, Lavatera olbia 'Rosea' forms a dense conical shape that is covered in a superb display of flowers from top to bottom.

Cutting back lavatera

Avoid cutting back old stems until the worst frosts are over, as pruning stimulates new growth that is easily damaged by freezing.

2 *By mid-spring, new growth will be apparent near the base of the plant. Cut off the old stems close to ground level.*

1 *During the winter, old stems become woody and dark colored. They protect the plant in cold conditions, but if not removed in mid-spring, they soon make the plant look leggy and untidy.*

3 *All that remains will be a small rosettelike cluster of young leaves virtually sitting on the ground. Strong new shoots will quickly grow from these to bear the current summer's flowers.*

Magnolia

Magnolias are the aristocrats of flowering shrubs: expensive, fussy and likely to sulk if they are not happy. However, a well-suited specimen in full flower is such a magnificent sight that it is well worth taking the trouble to get everything right. The ideal site is a garden with reasonably good, moisture-retentive (but not wet) lime-free soil (acid to neutral), with shelter and full sun or very light partial shade. *Magnolia stellata* is the easiest to accommodate, as it does not mind a little chalk. Being compact and bushy rather than big and treelike, it is also the most suitable for a small garden. *Magnolia* x *soulangeana* is the popular tree magnolia, with traditional off-white, tulip-shaped flowers, though named varieties with pink, mauve-streaked or very large flowers are sometimes available. These make good specimen trees for the middle of a lawn, but need space and lime-free soil. Avoid the evergreen *M. grandiflora* (with leaves rather like rhododendron leaves and huge white flowers in midsummer) unless you have plenty of room and time to wait. It makes a huge tree, often trained as a wall shrub up the sides of old houses, and rarely flowers for fifteen years or more.

Cultivars such as 'Exmouth' and 'Goliath' are faster to bloom but can still take ten years. Whichever you decide on, add plenty of organic matter before planting a magnolia, and once in place leave well alone. Established magnolias rarely if ever transplant successfully and do not take kindly to pruning. Magnolias are difficult to propagate and young plants slow to reach saleable size, hence their high price in nurseries. However, it is worth paying a little extra for a really outstanding cultivar.

Above: If you are looking for a compact magnolia to grow on slightly alkaline soil, then Magnolia loebneri *'Leonard Messel' is the perfect choice . The plant resembles* Magnolia stellata, *but with pink flowers.*

Left: A hybrid of uncertain parentage, M. x kewensis *'Wada's Memory' was named after the man who originally raised the batch of seed from which it was selected. The shape is characteristic of any good tree magnolia.*

Magnolia hypoleuca *'Jane' is a relatively new hybrid with elegant dark buds that open to medium-sized mauve flowers.*

Magnolia x soulangeana *'Pickard's Sundew' is an unusual and rarely seen cultivar with exceptionally large, waterlily-like flowers.*

Magnolia x loebneri *'Leonard Messel', a compact hybrid, is happy on slightly chalky soils.*

Magnolia x soulangeana *'Burgundy' is a pink and mauve variety of this popular species, which normally has the palest pink-tinged, off-white flowers.*

Magnolia stellata *'Rosea' is a good pink form of the popular and easily grown star magnolia. Good for small gardens and slightly chalky soils.*

Magnolia stellata *is the best magnolia for a small garden, as plants remain compact and bushy. Tolerates slightly chalky soils.*

Left: *Of the commonly available species, Magnolia* grandiflora *is the odd one out. It has evergreen leaves, and flowers in late summer. Plants take many years before they start flowering and, except in the mildest regions, are best grown against a wall that receives full sun at midday.*

Right: *Magnolia x* soulangeana *is widely known for its pale pink, tulip-shaped flowers stained purplish mauve at the base. It prefers lime-free soil and will not grow on shallow chalky soils.*

Mahonia

Mahonias are best known for their large, leathery, evergreen leaves, dramatic 'architectural' shapes and winter flowers, but each of the popular kinds has its own personality. *Mahonia aquifolium* is the most familiar; although not the most striking species, it is one of the most useful, as it grows happily in conditions few other shrubs tolerate - dry, shady soil under trees. Its low, spreading habit makes good weed-smothering ground cover, the holly-like foliage takes on purplish or bronzey tints in winter, and the spring flowers make loose yellow bunches at the tips of the shoots. Its hybrid 'Winter Sun' has specially good, scented flowers. 'Atropurpurea' has the best foliage color. *Mahonia japonica* and *M.* x *media* 'Charity' make good specimen shrubs for a site in weak sun or light shade. Each plant produces a few strong upright stems with large leaves arranged round them, each topped in winter and early spring by a starburst of spikes of yellow lily-of-the-valley-scented flowers. These look specially good as the centerpiece of a winter display, teamed with gold-variegated evergreens, such as *Euonymus* 'Emerald 'n' Gold' or *Hedera helix* 'Goldheart' (ivy), and underplanted with early daffodils. With long-lasting, weather-proof flowers, mahonias thrive in any reasonable garden soil and rarely need attention.

Above: The rarely seen cultivar, Mahonia x media *'Roundwood' has exceptionally large, bright, multi-story racemes of flower that appear from ruffs of prickly evergreen foliage.*

Right: Mahonia x media *'Winter Sun' is famous for its prolific flowering, with long racemes of lily-of-the-valley scented blooms. Any well-drained soil in sun or light dappled shade suits it.*

Tidying mahonia

Stems of young mahonia plants are often leggy and uneven in length. Before planting them, trim back out-of-shape shoots, but avoid hard pruning, which can be fatal. On mature plants, cut out leggy old stems to ground level in spring, but avoid denuding the plant.

Right: Mahonia aquifolium (Oregon grape) *is less striking than other members of the family, but is a very useful ground cover shrub for difficult parts of the garden. It tolerates poor soil, dry conditions and deep shade under trees.*

Left: Mahonia x media 'Charity' *makes a medium to large shrub, with upright stems topped with a spray of evergreen foliage resembling giant holly leaves, and in winter a cartwheel of fragrant yellow flowers.*

Right: *The fruits of mahonia are clusters of blue-black berries; this is* Mahonia japonica, *a species with unbranched stems, whose foliage often takes on attractive red and yellow tints during the winter.*

Malus - crab apples

Choosing a tree that will not outgrow its welcome in a small garden can be quite a problem. Crab apples are an excellent choice. They look like proper trees but simply stay small. Look for those grafted onto dwarfing rootstocks (the same as are used for fruit trees), since plants raised this way quickly grow to their full size and then stop. As well as making proper tree shapes in the garden, crab apples put on a substantial show of pink fruit-blossom in spring, followed by heavy crops of colorful fruits in late summer and fall. These vary in shape, size and color according to the cultivar, though none look much like culinary apples. 'Golden Hornet' produces many small, round, yellow fruits that hang on the tree well into winter before dropping off. 'John Downie', which has large, flask-shaped crimson-flushed yellow fruit, is the one to grow for making crab apple jelly, while 'Dartmouth' has small, purplish fruits. Plenty of less well-known varieties are available, too. There is also whole a

group of *Malus* cultivars, loosely known as purple-leaved crabs, which are grown for their coppery purple foliage; this offsets the deep pink blossom to perfection. However, these either do not fruit at all or produce such insignificant fruit that the foliage and flowers are the main reason for growing them. Crab apples like well-drained soil in full sun, and though they are not too fussy about windy areas, the blossom lasts longer in a sheltered spot. However, avoid a site that receives the early morning sun; just like normal fruit trees, flowers will brown and fruit crops will be ruined if the sun falls on frozen flowers early in spring.

Above: This ornamental crab apple is not growing on a dwarfing rootstock, but most sold nowadays are, so they tend to make smaller, more upright shapes.

Below: The fruit of Malus 'Golden Hornet' lasts on the tree well into winter, untouched by birds. Brown rot can 'mummify' old fruit on this decorative tree.

Above: Seen in close-up, the flowers of culinary apple trees are just as attractive as the ornamental crab apples, with the promise of an edible harvest. This cultivar is 'Sunset'.

Below: Malus 'Royalty' is an unusual cultivar with purple-tinged foliage, very deep pink blossom and wine red fruit. Unlike many crab apples, it retains its color all season.

Left: Malus 'John Downie' is the most popular crab apple cultivar for making crab apple jelly, which is rich rosy-salmon color. Pick the fruit in early fall, as it soon drops from the tree.

Above: A standard-trained crab apple of any species, in full flower, makes a striking garden specimen. Trees need a sunny situation with reasonable shelter as the blossom does not last long in windy weather.

Philadelphus

Philadelphus flowers in early midsummer, producing white blooms that waft a haunting fragrance of orange blossom over the garden. Several varieties are available, with either single or double flowers; the best known is 'Virginal', which has double flowers. One cultivar, *P. coronarius* 'Aureus', is grown as much for its bright golden spring foliage as the flowers, which are a little less plentifully produced than in other cultivars. Philadelphus are good, tough, grow-anywhere shrubs for sun or light shade; they tolerate polluted air, poor soil and indifferent cultivation, and are generally problem-free. They are one of the dozen or so 'essential' shrubs that you can guarantee to find in most gardens, but as with many common plants they are often neglected, allowed to grow tall and straggling, cluttered with old stems that no longer flower well. If cut down hard - a common response to try and curtail excess size - they simply respond by throwing up enormously tall, thin, sappy shoots that do not flower for years and make the plant look even worse than before. The solution is two-fold. Firstly, only plant *Philadelphus* where there is enough room. Most of them make shrubby bushes at least 6ft(1.8m) high and 4-5ft(1.2-1.5m) across, though 'Virginal' grows over 10ft(3m) high and 5-6ft (1.5-1.8m) across. If space is a problem, choose the naturally compact *P. coronarius* 'Variegatus' with its highly attractive cream and cream-marked leaves, or the diminutive *P. lewisii* 'Manteau d'Hermine', a very compact dwarf shrub that grows to about 3ft (90cm) high with fragrant, double creamy-white flowers. Secondly, prune them properly. The aim is to remove old stems in succession and encourage new branches to form from the base, to take over future flowering. Do not remove more than one fifth of the stems at any one time; the plant will only compensate by growing more than ever.

Below: 'Belle Etoile' is a relatively compact cultivar that grows to about 6ft(1.8m) high. The single flowers - large by comparison with others of the group - are highly scented.

Pruning

Prune philadelphus every year immediately after flowering. Cut back the flowered stems to their junction with an older shoot, distinguishable by its darker colored bark. Improve old plants by completely removing a few of the oldest, most unproductive branches from the base.

1 Cut back long and out-of-shape shoots to their junction with a more compact branch. Avoid cutting back too hard, otherwise the plant will produce long, straight, non-flowering shoots.

Below: P. coronarius 'Aureus' has gold new foliage in spring, which contrasts with the creamy-white scented flowers in early summer. The foliage later fades to a dull lime green.

2 *Although not perfect, the shape is better. During the subsequent growing season, new shoots arising from near the base will produce a good framework and bushier plant.*

Left: 'Virginal' is probably the best double-flowered cultivar ever developed. The flowers are large, packed with petals, long-lasting and highly scented. It can also be cut and put in a vase indoors.

Above: P. tomentosus 'Virginal' can reach almost 10ft(3m) high. This makes it a good choice for the back of a large border or as a specimen shrub in a spot where it has plenty of room to develop fully.

Pieris

The dramatic, red, poinsettia-like heads of pieris may look like flowers, but this is just an illusion. They are actually the young leaves that are temporarily very brightly colored. True pieris flowers appear at the same time; these are the small white bells, arranged in rows and growing from the tip of older shoots that carried the previous year's bracts. But however you think of them, their impact is tremendous. Pieris stands out well when the garden is still recovering from the after-effects of winter, in early or mid-spring. The first to perform are cultivars of *Pieris japonica*. These have copper-colored young foliage, and some varieties have flowers (as against young leaves) in colors other than white. The best known of these is probably 'Valley Valentine', with its bunches of purplish red flowers. *Pieris formosa* cultivars grow about half as big again as japonica types, but these are the ones with the brightest red young leaves; their flowers are usually white. Variegated forms of pieris are also available, and make specially striking shrubs for a 'key' spot. Pieris are slow-growing, evergreen shrubs that eventually reach medium to large size; they cannot be kept small by pruning, so only plant them where there is enough room to let them mature. They need similar conditions to rhododendrons - acid soil and slight shade. However, pieris will grow in a more open situation, provided it is sheltered from cold winds and shaded by other plants from the early morning sun, which in early spring would otherwise damage the young flowers and colored foliage. Chlorosis (yellowing foliage) is the result of lime locking up iron chemically in the soil. Check that the soil is sufficiently acid and feed plants with a product containing sequestered iron each spring.

Left: *Generally, pieris do not need pruning, but check plants periodically and cut out any dead, broken or unhealthy looking stems whenever you see them. Remove all-green shoots from variegated varieties to prevent stronger green shoots 'taking over'.*

Pieris in tubs

Being slow-growing and naturally compact, pieris make very good subjects for growing in tubs, especially if the garden soil is unsuitable. With its abundant flowers, Pieris japonica 'Valley Valentine', shown here, does well in a container and brings color to the garden in late winter.

Below: *The foliage of this pieris is turning yellow due to chlorosis. It will quickly recover when repotted into fresh ericaceous potting mix, which is suitable for lime-hating plants.*

Below: *Nowadays, nurseries and garden centers stock a wide range of pieris, especially in areas with acid soil, where the plants naturally thrive.*

Pieris japonica 'Dorothy Wyckoff'

Feeding pieris

Pieris buds are initiated in late summer and fall, when the plants need plenty of moisture. A high-potash feed (e.g. liquid tomato feed) at this time promotes good flower the following spring.

Pieris japonica 'Grayswood'

Pieris floribunda 'Forest Flame'

Pieris japonica 'Mountain Fire'

Pieris japonica 'White Rim'

Pieris 'Flaming Silver'

Potentilla

Because of its small size, *Potentilla* is often regarded more as a flower than a shrub, although that is what it actually is. This bushy, free-flowering plant belongs to the rose family, and close-up its flowers do indeed look like small, wide-open, single wild roses, but in all the 'hot' bright colors - yellow, orange, pink and red, plus white, depending on the cultivar. *Potentilla* foliage is small and ferny and supported by wiry stems that build up into neat, dense hillocks, studded with flower from early to late summer. Most cultivars grow to about 24in(60cm) high, although taller and shorter kinds can be found. Potentillas will grow in quite poor soils, including chalky or sandy ones, as long as they are well drained. Most do best in sun, although some of the red shades fade fast in full sun and are best given very light shade. Potentillas mingle especially well with rock plants, which enjoy similar conditions, and are much used on banks, raised beds, hollow-topped walls and for the front of shrub borders. They also mix well with herbaceous flowers provided they are not overcrowded; slugs and snails can be a problem in this situation. Their small, finely cut foliage and 'solid' flowers associate particularly well with large-leaved foliage plants and those with upright flower spikes in complementary colors; *Heuchera*, *Crocosmia* or *Kniphofia* (red hot pokers) make good partners. Or use them as a flowering carpet in front of deep glossy green evergreen shrubs, such as *Arbutus unedo* or *Fatsia japonica*, or purple-leaved kinds, such as *Cotinus coggygria* or the purple forms of *Cordyline* or *Phormium*, for a specially striking display.

Above: *Red-flowered potentillas are rather prone to fading in the sun, so these cultivars are best grown in very light dappled shade to preserve the color. This is Potentilla fruticosa 'Red Ace', a very popular cultivar.*

P. fruticosa 'Tangerine' forms a low, mound-shaped spreading plant with coppery yellow flowers; the color lasts best when the plant is grown in light shade, otherwise it fades.

P. fruticosa 'Goldfinger' is a larger, more upright cultivar that can reach 3ft(90cm) high, with deep golden flowers.

P. fruticosa 'Abbotswood' has a dwarf compact shape with dark foliage that offsets the freely produced white flowers.

P. fruticosa 'Primrose Beauty' is a spreading cultivar with gray-green foliage. The pale yellow flowers have a deeper yellow eye in the center.

64

Right: The shrubby cinquefoil, P. fruticosa, thrives in sun on rocky, often chalky, well-drained soil. Its hybrids enjoy similar conditions, although orange- and red-flowered cultivars tend to fade in strong sun, so are best grown in light shade.

Pruning potentilla

As soon as all the flowers are finished each year, clip the plants over with shears. This 'haircut' removes most of the dead flower heads and reshapes the plants, which become straggly. Do not cut into old, dark-colored wood.

Raising new plants from cuttings

Take cuttings from the older stems of potentilla in midsummer. Tear a few sideshoots from the sunny side of the bush (without spoiling the look of the plant). Once cuttings have rooted, pot them individually into small pots and keep them well watered until they are large enough to plant in the garden.

2 Push several cuttings in around the side of a pot of seed mix. Water in well to firm the mixture slightly round the cuttings.

3 Slip a plastic bag over the pot to prevent drying out. Rooting will take 8-10 weeks. After about 6 weeks, make a few small holes in the bag and remove it entirely after 8 weeks to acclimatize the foliage.

Below: Potentilla fruticosa 'Princess' grows rather larger than many potentillas and makes a tall hillock-shaped plant about 30in(75cm) tall and the same across. It has delicate pink flowers over 1in(2.5cm) across.

1 Take 2-3in(5-7.5cm)-long side-shoots and strip off the leaves from the bottom half of each shoot. Make a clean cut across the base, leaving no dangling shreds of bark.

Prunus - shrubby varieties

Mention *Prunus* and most people immediately think of flowering cherries. Yet there are plenty of surprisingly versatile bushy species, both evergreen and deciduous. The evergreen species are commonly called laurels and are usually grown as hedges. Since the leaves are so large, they are usually pruned rather than clipped formally. (Take care with the clippings of *Prunus laurocerasus*, as the leaves are poisonous, though the toxins break down when composted and will not harm other plants mulched with them). Although the laurels flower, the blooms are white and not terribly exciting. Another group, known as wild cherries, are the very first *Prunus* species to flower. They have small, delicate, single flowers that are subtle but very pretty. The plants are very versatile; they can be pruned to make informal country hedges, planted in rows as shelter belts or allowed to grow up into small trees in wild gardens. Here, they provide nesting and perching places for birds, as well as late summer and fall fruit for them. Wild cherries grow in a range of situations, but dislike acid soil and shade. For normal borders, more conventional mid-spring-flowering shrubby species grow well in most reasonable garden conditions, given good drainage and a sunny situation. Dual-purpose prunus can be grown either as a small tree or medium to large shrub, depending on how they were originally trained. (It is possible to convert one to the other while the plant is young, but it is not always very successful - much simpler to buy the shape you want in the first place.) These include *Prunus incisa* (the Mount Fuji cherry) and *Prunus cistena*, which has purple foliage and small, single pink flowers. *Prunus triloba* (double pink rosette-like blooms) is more tender than it is usually given credit for, and is best grown trained flat against a wall in all but the mildest regions. In a really mild climate it makes a good tree.

Choosing a prunus

Select a plant with plenty of branches for maximum flower. Since many types have a slightly loose, open habit of growth, a plant with a poor branch structure will only get worst as it grows, unless you first retrain it. This means cutting it down almost to ground level in early spring to make it branch out from the base, but you will not get any flowers that year.

GOOD PLANT
A fairly symmetrical shape, with plenty of well-spaced branches from the base.

BAD PLANT
Lopsided, with only a few poorly positioned branches and little growth from the base.

Above: Prunus glandulosa 'Sinensis', the Chinese bush cherry, needs a warm sheltered spot; in cold areas, it is best trained against a wall. Stems can be cut and forced into flower early in a vase in a warm room indoors.

Right: *The dwarf Russian almond, Prunus tenella 'Fire Hill', starts as a bushy plant, as seen here, but once established, spreads by suckers that 'run' through a bed, creating a loose informal haze of flower in spring. It looks great among naturalized spring bulbs.*

Below: *P. laurocerasus 'Otto Luyken' is a much more compact form of cherry laurel, reaching only about 4ft(1.2m), but with similar flowers and very glossy foliage. Use it for low hedges or as deep, weed-smothering ground cover.*

Above: *The cherry laurel, Prunus laurocerasus, has large, rather rhododendron-like evergreen foliage and flowers in mid-spring. White candle-shaped heads of bloom are followed by berries. Makes a tall hedge or screen.*

Prunus subhirtella 'Autumnalis' grown as a bush instead of a tree. Here it is flowering in early spring.

Prunus glandulosa 'Sinensis' in tight bud. It flowers in late spring.

67

Prunus - flowering cherries

Flowering cherries are the trees that everyone, even the least gardening-minded, can usually identify with ease. The best known are the Japanese cherries, which have masses of showy double blossom in late spring or early summer. However, like lilac, the flower tends to be shortlived, especially in an exposed area, and the trees do not usually contribute much to the decoration of the garden for the rest of the time. Many kinds can also get far too big for small gardens, such as the notorious 'Kanzan', and are much better suited to parks and similar situations. At maturity (about 30 years old) Japanese cherry trees can start to decline, suffering from disease and shoot dieback. If this happens they are best replaced, as flowering is reduced and no treatment seems to help. (To avoid the possible carry-over of root diseases, replant the space with a tree from a different family and improve the soil well first.) However, some of the smaller Japanese cherries, such as 'Cheal's Weeping Cherry' and the compact upright 'Amanogawa', are ideal for gardens and do not seem so prone to problems. There are also other species of flowering cherries entirely. Specially lovely are the fall-flowering cherry,

Prunus subhirtella 'Autumnalis', and the various forms of weeping spring cherry, *Prunus subhirtella* 'Pendula', which flowers early in the year. All flowering cherry trees need a chalky, well-drained soil and sun to thrive; a sheltered situation helps the flowers to last longer. Buy well-trained trees of reasonable size from a reliable supplier. Avoid pruning if possible, due to the risk of disease entering the sap stream. If needed at all - to remove damaged, out-of-place or congested branches and generally tidy the shape - pruning should be done in late summer.

Left: 'Amanogawa' is one of the most upright-growing and compact of flowering cherries, which makes it ideal for smaller gardens. It flowers reliably well every year, in early summer.

Windy situations

Flowering cherries need a warm, sheltered spot in the sun to be seen at their best, as the flowers open early in the season and are relatively large and fragile. In an exposed site, the blossom - the main attraction of the plant - is often blown off the tree almost as soon as it opens. The later flowering kinds will fare better, as the weather can be expected to improve as spring progresses.

Prunus subhirtella 'Autumnalis', the autumn-flowering cherry, is normally grown as a tree, with a distinct trunk.

Occasionally, you may find bushy plants, which can be allowed to develop as a big bushy shrub instead.

Right: P. subhirtella 'Pendula', *a weeping cherry, makes a spectacular medium-sized tree. It flowers in early spring. A deep pink version is also available.*

Below: 'Cheal's Weeping Cherry' *does not occupy as wide an area as many weeping trees, so it suits a small garden. Pink blooms in late spring.*

Below: P. sargentii *has richly colored, shiny bark and wide spreading branches that create a broad canopy. The rich pink flowers associate beautifully with bronzey young foliage and the fall color is also good.*

'Pink Shell' is a small, elegant tree with gracefully drooping branches that bear pale shell-pink flowers in late spring.

'Spire' is a tall, narrow tree with pale pink flowers and leaves that take on autumnal tints before falling.

Rhododendron

There are few sights so spectacular as woodland gardens full of rhododendrons in full flower in early summer. However, there are also plenty of compact kinds that are ideal for small gardens among other plants or even in containers. Dwarf rhododendrons, such as yakushimanum hybrids, are the most suitable for small gardens; deciduous rhododendrons (once called deciduous azaleas) also tend to be reasonably sized, and there are plenty of small and medium-sized evergreen kinds that do not outgrow their welcome. Always check sizes before buying. To flourish, rhododendrons must have acid soil and light dappled shade, best provided by a light canopy of trees, such as birches or pines. If the garden soil is not naturally acid, grow compact kinds in containers of ericaceous potting mix or in a specially prepared isolated peat bed. (Adding peat to normal or chalky soil is not enough - the plants will not thrive.) Keep them well fed and watered. When grown in garden soil, rhododendrons need reasonably good drainage, but never allow them to dry out in summer. This is particularly important in mid- to late summer, when the buds that will open out into the following year's flowers are forming. If the soil is dry then, buds abort and plants miss flowering for a year.

'Bow Bells'

The rhododendrons featured below are all compact cultivars.

'Eider'

'Scarlet Wonder'

'Vuyk's Scarlet'

Frost damage

The buds - especially those of earlier flowering cultivars - can be damaged by late frost, just as they start to open. Frosted buds fail to develop, so pick them off. Tightly closed buds should escape; do not remove them.

Right: Most large-flowered rhododendron hybrids are grafted onto rootstocks of wild R. ponticum. *If an odd purple flower appears, suspect a sucker. Trace it back to the root and tear it out or it will soon 'take over'.*

'Blue Star'

'Curlew'

'Hatsugin'

Watering and feeding a rhododendron

1 Water rhododendrons in well after planting. As their roots remain close to the surface, keep them well watered during dry spells, even when they are well established.

2 Rhododendrons benefit from a regular feed in spring as new growth starts. Special feeds for these and other acid-loving plants are ideal for pots or plants in the ground.

3 Keep plants well watered in midsummer and add a dose of liquid tomato feed. This is high in potash and will encourage bud formation at the tips of the shoots.

4 After watering well in spring, mulch around rhododendrons with 1in(2.5cm) of chipped bark, moss peat or, as here, cocoa shell, all of which are slightly acidic.

Ribes - flowering currant

Flowering currant is an old cottage garden favorite that is fast getting a new look. First, the range of colors is extending, as the traditional pink-flowered *Ribes sanguineum* cultivars are joined by white-flowered cultivars and a gold-leaved form. (This one has pink flowers, which some may think clash with the foliage.) Secondly, the shape of the plant is changing; ribes are now sometimes grown as small standards or fans, ideal for small gardens as they take up less room than a normal bushy plant. There is no reason why flowering currants should not be trained as wall shrubs, cordons and even more elaborate shapes, too. Training is fun and easy to do with such a fast-growing and obliging plant. Since cuttings root easily, it is not difficult to set aside a few plants on which to try out training techniques, and keep only the best. Finally, other sorts of ribes are beginning to appear on the scene. Besides the original *Ribes sanguineum*, a couple of unusual species, once hardly seen, are now sometimes available. The buffalo currant *(Ribes odoratum)* has clove-scented, yellow flowers in spring and fall-tinted foliage, while the most striking of all is *Ribes speciosum*, which is more like a thornless gooseberry bush in shape, with elegant, long, dangly, brilliant red flowers. These are something like a particularly good fuchsia species, with a dash of hummingbird thrown in!

Below: R. sanguineum 'White Icicle' *(left) is a new variety, with white flowers. It grows less strongly than the pink- and red-flowered kinds. Gold-leaved* R. sanguineum 'Brocklebankii' *(middle) is rather slow growing. Ribes sanguineum 'Porky's Pink' (right), also a new variety, has bright pink flowers.*

Use very sharp secateurs or a small pair of scissors to cut away unwanted material. Avoid tearing or damaging the stem and take care not to remove the wrong bits; think before you cut!

1 *To train a standard flowering currant, either root your own cutting or try to find a single-stemmed plant in a nursery. Cut the tip of the stem off at the required height.*

Ribes speciosum *is a highly unusual and attractive variety.*

After nipping out the tips of the growing shoots three or four times, a good 'head' will have developed. From then on, only trim to shape immediately after flowering. Do not prune at other times, or the following year's flowers will be lost.

2 *If the stem is less than pencil thick, remove only the sideshoots. Remove the leaves a year later when it has become thick enough to support the weight of the 'head'.*

3 *If the plant has a thicker stem, remove both leaves and sideshoots. This will encourage all the energy to go into the sideshoots at the top of the stem, which will form the 'head'.*

4 *Leave only the top five sideshoots. Pinch out their growing tips when they are 2-3in(5-7.5cm) long. Nip out the growing tips of subsequent sideshoots at 2-3in(5-7.5cm) long.*

5 *Keep well fed and watered, and in a sheltered spot in some sun until the head is well formed, when the tree can be planted out. It is worth tying the stem to a stake for extra support.*

Rosa - shrubby varieties

One group of roses - shrub roses - have a place here, since they are treated as flowering shrubs and not like conventional roses. Shrub roses have flowers quite unlike those of hybrid teas and floribundas. Commonly known as 'wild' roses, they are grown for their prickly stems, foliage and rosehips, as much as for the flowers. The flowers are often produced over a period lasting only six to eight weeks, which makes them suitable for growing in mixed borders amongst other seasonal flowers. Unlike modern roses, shrub roses rarely suffer from diseases such as mildew, so they do not need constant spraying and little or no pruning, making them ideal for a low-maintenance garden. The permanent thicket of prickly stems makes shrub roses ideal for growing in front borders or as boundary hedges, to deter intruders, pets and livestock. Some of the species make enormous plants quite unsuited to small gardens, but with care some very attractive compact kinds can be found. Where space is short, consider shrub roses grafted onto a tall stem to make a standard 'tree' shape for the back of a border or as a specimen plant in a lawn. 'Canary Bird' and 'Ballerina' are often grown this way, but most spectacular are the ground cover roses, such as 'Nozomi', whose lax habit makes a most attractive weeping shape.

Left: Rosa rubrifolia, *now renamed* Rosa glauca, *is a great favorite with flower arrangers. Its pewter-colored foliage persists throughout the growing season and the single pink flowers are followed by small red hips.*

Right: The shrub rose 'Ballerina' flowers continuously all summer, has a good musky perfume and makes a naturally neat, compact bush, suitable for a small garden. It also makes a most attractive standard plant.

Encouraging hips

Shrub roses generally need little pruning. Many, such as Rosa rugosa *and* moyesii, *produce large rosehips; do not deadhead them or hips will not form.*

Left: Trim over-long shoots and remove dead stems when you see them.

Below: Most rugosa cultivars have large single flowers and hips. This is 'Frau Dagmar Hastrup'.

Above: Rosa moyesii 'Geranium' is valued for its long, flask-shaped, bright orange rosehips. However. the flowers and foliage are also most attractive. The prickly stems mesh together to make a good barrier.

Right: 'Canary Bird' is another very popular shrub rose. It is one of the earliest to flower, in mid-spring, several weeks ahead of the others, and is available as both bush and standard forms. It tolerates light shade.

Above: 'Nozomi', a ground cover rose, makes a wonderful weeping standard when grafted onto a short trunk; grow it to add height to a border, as a small specimen 'tree' or in a container. The pearly pink flowers are not scented.

General care

Roses prefer heavy retentive soil; clays and loams suit them well. On light soils, dig in plenty of well-rotted manure before planting to improve the soil's water-holding capacity, and mulch heavily each spring. Apply an annual dose of rose fertilizer in spring. Shrub roses generally need little pruning other than to keep them in shape. Many have loose floppy habits; tie them up to stakes to keep them tidy. Deadhead plants on a weekly basis during the flowering period.

1 To keep plants at their best, snip off dead flower heads as individual blooms go over. Remove the dead flower complete with a short length of stem, cutting to just above a leaf joint.

2 When the last blooms are over, remove all the remaining dead flowers in one go. At the same time, slightly shorten any shoots that are sticking out and spoiling the shape.

3 After the final deadheading and light summer pruning, the head should make a neat spherical shape. Remove any dead twigs and other debris to complete the job.

Sambucus

The ornamental elders are some of our most underrated shrubs. Cultivars of the wild elder *(Sambucus nigra)* are the toughest of all and tolerate dreadful conditions, such as windy sites, wet clay soil, impoverished sand and total neglect. Yet they flower happily, producing the typical wide, flat-topped, white clusters of wild elder, although the fruit is not usually very reliable. (The fruit of some ornamental elders is not safe to eat; use special fruiting cultivars for culinary purposes.) Cultivars of *S. racemosa* are the ones most commonly recommended for the garden, as they include the frillier foliage kinds, although this group will not tolerate poor conditions; give them reasonable garden soil and shelter from cold winds. A site in sun for at least half the day is best for all elders; they will tolerate some shade, but neither the flowers nor the foliage grow so well in poor light. Yellow-leaved cultivars need sun all day to develop their full color. Left alone, elders quickly grow into characterful small trees with craggy bark and eccentric shapes that look just right in wildlife gardens, country hedges or cottage gardens. Since elders accept heavy pruning, their shape can be tailored to taste. (Do not worry about making a mistake - elder grows back so fast it permits a second attempt within a year or two.) Starting with a small nursery plant, it is quite easy for anyone without previous experience of tree pruning or training to turn elders into reasonably conventional trees, as well as flowering or foliage bushes.

Above: *In full sun,* S. nigra *'Purpurea' produces fine, deep purple leaves. Being naturally twiggy, a large elder with a bushy shape is a good support for clematis and other climbers.*

Right: Sambucus nigra *adds a natural touch to a wild or country garden, especially when it grows up through a hedge, such as this hawthorn. It grows this way naturally in country hedges.*

Pruning sambucus

To grow as a small tree, choose a plant with one stem, or remove the weakest stems from a bushy plant, leaving a single, strong, straight, upright one. Gradually remove a few lower branches every spring until you have a clean trunk of the required height. Allow the top of the tree to branch out, but prune to keep it a fairly symmetrical shape.

1 *For a conventional shrub, cut back the stems quite hard every 2-3 years in mid-spring. Cut all the stems back to about 2ft(60cm) above ground level.*

2 *If a variegated elder produces all gold or, more commonly, all green shoots, remove the 'wrong' shoots at once. Vigorous, all-green shoots will soon dominate a plant.*

Left: With its deeply cut, bright golden foliage, Sambucus racemosa 'Plumosa Aurea' is one of the most stunning elders. After a good summer, it is also decorated with clusters of bright red berries.

Right: Sambucus nigra *'Aurea' is the perfect choice for gold foliage in a sunny but exposed spot with poor drainage. Cut it down hard in spring every second or third year for extra-large foliage.*

Right: Variegated elders look choice, but if they are cultivars of wild elder, they are surprisingly tough. This is the green-and-white S. nigra *'Albovariegata'. Cream-green variegated and all-gold cultivars are available, too.*

Skimmia

Skimmia japonica 'Foremanii'. The female form produces berries if there is a male nearby.

Skimmia japonica 'Fragrans'. Male form grown for greenish buds. Scented white flowers open in late spring. No berries.

Skimmia is an incredibly useful shrub that is only just becoming well known. Plants are neat, compact evergreens that are at the height of their display in winter. In most forms, male and female flowers grow on separate plants; only female flowers develop berries, while male varieties have the more spectacular flowers, so choose a cultivar of the right sex for the sort of display you want. But what looks most spectacular is to grow the pair up through each other; this way you get what looks like a single shrub with both berries and bunches of buds. If you only have room for one variety, look for *Skimmia reevesiana*, which has both sexes on one plant, so always sets berries. Skimmias are slightly fussy about soil. Grow them in neutral or acid soil, in sun or light shade, in a border with plants that won't swamp the skimmia; heathers, *Arbutus unedo* and other ericaceous plants make good partners. Because they are at their best from late fall to early spring, skimmias are wonderful plants for winter tubs. Use ericaceous potting mix, and grow male and female forms in the same container. In spring, you can plant them out into the garden, or keep them fed and watered during the summer to use as background foliage with pots of summer flowers.

Skimmia japonica 'Rubella'. Male form grown for large, pyramidal bunches of pink buds in winter. These develop slowly into off-white flowers by late spring.

Above: Since male and female flowers grow on separate plants, you need one of each if the female is to bear berries. Grow them fairly close together to ensure pollination - no more than 50ft(15m) apart, ideally closer.

Skimmia reevesiana. A hermaphrodite form that produces berries even when grown alone.

Right: Skimmias enjoy light shade and acid soil, so they thrive in the company of rhododendrons. Other ericaceous plants also look good with them; in sun, grow them with heathers.

Left: This is Skimmia reevesiana, *a hermaphrodite form that produces both male and female flowers on the same plant. This means that it does not need another variety to be grown nearby as a pollinator.*

Above: Skimmias can be used to make *striking plant associations with others that like acid soils. Here, Skimmia* japonica *'Rubella', a male form grown for its big clusters of flowers, makes a good contrast with* Pieris.

A skimmia in a tub

Line a wooden tub with plastic, cut a drainage hole in the liner and part-fill the tub with ericaceous potting mix. Sit the plant in the center of the tub and firm it down gently. The top of the rootball should be about 1in(2.5cm) below the rim of the container. Fill the gap around the rootball with more mix, again firming it down lightly. Site the tub in a sheltered spot in weak sun or dappled shade. Avoid a spot in line with early morning sun. Water the tub and keep it moist but not waterlogged.

Spiraea

Every garden needs a basis of shrubs that flower reliably, virtually grow themselves and look good in borders among other plants, even if they do not particularly stand out as stars in their own right. Spiraeas belong to this category and there is a wide range to choose from. Those with white flowers are the first to bloom, producing masses of tiny white flowers in spring. Summer-flowering spiraeas have more color; heads of fluffy flowers, either in loose groups or in spikes, appear in various shades of pink from pale to mauve. They are specially good value, as the flowering season lasts from mid- to late summer. With so many different spiraeas available, it is not hard to find one that makes the right size for any given spot; they vary from very small to very large. Use them to bulk out borders; they associate well with herbaceous flowers and other shrubs, particularly when grown as part of a very varied mixture. They are ideal for creating a traditional mixed border look and being fast-growing, they are also perfect for filling new beds or giving an impression of 'instant' maturity to a new garden.

Spiraeas are not fussy plants; they grow in most garden soils, in sun or light shade. Like a lot of easily grown plants, spiraeas are often neglected and the plants fill up with dead twiggy growth that looks unattractive. This is easily prevented by proper pruning, which only becomes necessary after the plants are about five years old and dead twigs start to become apparent.

Above: Spiraea arguta, *a spring-flowering species, makes a medium-sized, arching shrub. It is inclined to be untidy, so prune to improve the shape after flowering if necessary.*

Below: S. japonica *'Golden Princess'. If you are not too keen on bright pink flowers with a gold background, prune hard each spring to promote strong foliage without the flowers.*

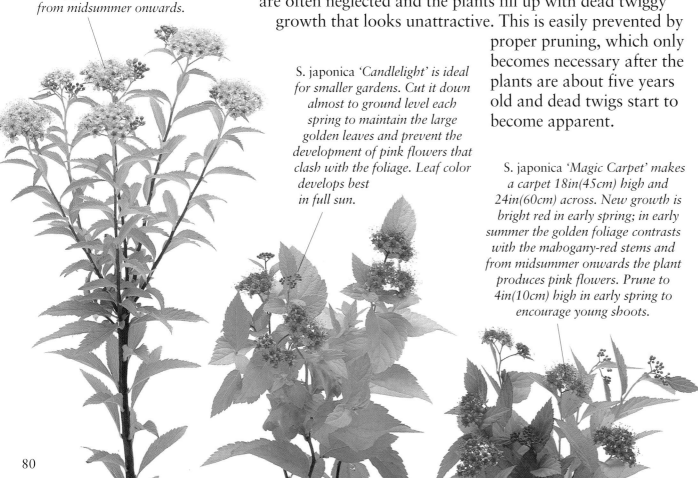

Spiraea 'Shirobana' makes an open spreading shrub, growing to about 4ft(1.2m), with flat heads of pink-and-white flowers from midsummer onwards.

S. japonica 'Candlelight' is ideal for smaller gardens. Cut it down almost to ground level each spring to maintain the large golden leaves and prevent the development of pink flowers that clash with the foliage. Leaf color develops best in full sun.

S. japonica 'Magic Carpet' makes a carpet 18in(45cm) high and 24in(60cm) across. New growth is bright red in early spring; in early summer the golden foliage contrasts with the mahogany-red stems and from midsummer onwards the plant produces pink flowers. Prune to 4in(10cm) high in early spring to encourage young shoots.

Above: *If cut down hard each spring, the foliage of S. japonica 'Goldflame' is a stunning combination of orange, bronze and gold. If allowed to flower, as here, the foliage becomes very dull.*

Below: *Bridal wreath, Spiraea arguta, makes a simple but stunning background for a variety of spring flowers in a border. The plant arches naturally to create a weeping effect.*

Pruning spiraea

Tidy older plants by cutting out a few of the oldest branches from low down in the plant each year. Do the spring-flowering (white) kinds when they finish flowering, and the summer-flowering (pink) kinds in mid-spring before they flower. Cut back spiraeas grown for their golden foliage to the ground in mid-spring.

1 *If you plant a spiraea in late summer, after the flowers are over, tidy it up first. Cut away the straggly growths from the base.*

2 *Use secateurs to deadhead the plant, cutting below each spent flower head to just above a young healthy shoot lower down the stem.*

3 *Cut back long straggly shoots that stick out beyond the outline of the plant to restore the shape. Cut just above a young shoot.*

4 *The final result is a shrub with a neat dome shape. All the old growth and other debris is removed along with the dead flower heads. You can repeat this type of tidying each year after the plants have flowered in the garden to encourage new young shoots.*

Syringa - lilac

The popular lilac featured on chocolate boxes and soap wrappers is French lilac, *Syringa vulgaris*, which has the familiar pyramidal spikes of heavily perfumed white, purple, wine-red or pinky-mauve flowers and heart-shaped leaves. Yet despite its wide appeal, it is not the reliable grow-anywhere plant you might expect. Lilac blooms for three weeks (at best) in early summer, often coinciding with a spell of wet or windy weather that finishes the display prematurely, so a well-sheltered site is essential if the rather delicate flowers are to last their full term. White lilacs are particularly prone to weather damage. Lilacs thrive anywhere except in acid conditions - they particularly favor chalky soils. But they are notoriously prone to suckering and unless suckers are removed regularly, the shrubs are rapidly overtaken by vigorous shoots arising from the underground rootstock and turn into untidy spreading bushes that no longer flower well. The best way to use lilacs is as big shrubs for the back of a large border, where the foliage acts as a foil to summer flowers for the rest of the season. And look out for species lilacs; these very attractive, free-flowering, medium-sized shrubs deserve wider recognition. Choose *Syringa* x *persica* (Persian lilac), which has fragrant lilac-colored flowers in late spring, or the bright pink panicles of *Syringa reflexa*.

Above: Syringa microphylla 'Superba', a medium to large species lilac, produces rose-pink blooms in late spring or early summer and continues to flower lightly through to early fall.

Below: French lilacs, such as this 'Congo', are grafted and normally produce suckers round the base. By growing them with a short trunk, as here, it is easy to tell which shoots are suckers and to remove them in time.

Left: Hybrid French lilacs are cultivars of Syringa vulgaris, *developed in France around 1900. They appear in a wide range of shades. This is 'Mme. Florent Stepman', which has creamy buds opening to white.*

Right: 'Masséna' *has particularly large and deeply colored panicles of flowers. Like all the hybrid French lilacs, it is very sweetly scented and the flower heads make a nearly perfect pyramidal shape.*

Above: Another species lilac, Syringa x persica *(Persian lilac) makes a dense, bushy, medium to large shrub that almost vanishes under its crop of scented flowers in early summer.*

Left: Like all hybrid French lilacs, the flowers of 'Président Grévyi' are good for cutting for indoor use. If windy weather threatens them, this is the best way of protecting open flowers.*

Species lilacs

Species lilacs are not as familiar as, and look quite different from, their well-known relatives. You may occasionally see them in garden centers, otherwise look for them in nurseries specializing in choice or unusual shrubs.

Viburnum

Viburnums are a large group of shrubs that between them provide a range of attractions for all seasons and all gardens. Each species is quite different from the rest. Some are grown for early spring flowers on bare stems, others for striking evergreen foliage, winter flowers, fall berries, scented flowers, or - the choicer kinds - for flat heads of lacecap flowers on tiered wedding-cake-shaped plants. Viburnums range in size from very small to very large and, depending on species, can be planted in borders, as specimen plants in lawns, as low-maintenance ground cover, in light dappled shade or woodland clearings, or in gardens designed to attract wildlife. The plants grow best in good, fertile garden soil that has had plenty of organic matter dug in first. Avoid extremes - of acidity or alkalinity, or very wet or dry soils. Most species do best in sun or light shade and are reasonably tolerant of wind and weather. However, the choicer *Viburnum plicatum* cultivars and the scented kinds, such as the early spring-flowering *Viburnum farreri*, *bodnantense* and mid- to late spring-flowering *carlesii*, are best grown in a sheltered site to protect their blooms and concentrate their perfume. Viburnums can be rather slow to establish and hence need good aftercare, so keep new plants watered in dry spells for the first summer. Once settled, they grow slowly but without problems - no pruning is needed except to remove dead or damaged shoots. The species grown for berries, such as *opulus* and *davidii*, need planting in groups for cross pollination to occur - if space is short, plant two together in the same planting hole so they grow up through each other.

Young viburnums

Young plants are often naturally a bit straggly; a light trim before planting will improve the shape and encourage the plant to develop a dense bushy shape.

This strong upright-growing branch spoils the symmetrical shape, so cut it off close to the base of the plant.

Right: *With its tiers of horizontal branches,* V. plicatum *'Mariesii' is a choice architectural plant, even when not in flower. The white flowers lie in rows along the tops of the branches, making them look as if covered in snow. Needs full sun and shelter.*

Right: V. davidii, *a compact, evergreen plant, produces striking turquoise berries if several plants are grown close together to ensure that cross pollination occurs.*

Below: V. opulus *'Sterile' has large round snowball-like clusters of flowers in spring. This is the best type of viburnum for growing in wet or boggy soil. It does not have berries.*

Pruning viburnum

Shorten long, straggly or out-of-shape branches of mature viburnum shrubs at any time of year, cutting back just above a group of side shoots that will grow out to give a bushier plant. Keep plants in shape by occasionally shortening over-long branches or any that are bare towards the tip.

Right: Check over established plants periodically and cut out any dead or diseased branches.

Viburnum tinus *is a popular, medium-sized, evergreen shrub that produces white, perfumed flowers from late fall to early spring. It tolerates light shade.*

Viburnum bodnantense *'Deben' is very similar to 'Dawn', except for its deeper pink flowers. Grow both varieties in a sheltered spot close to a doorway, where you can enjoy their scent in winter.*

Viburnum bodnantense *'Dawn' is best known for its very fragrant, pale pink clusters of flowers that appear on the bare stems throughout the winter. They stand up well to bad weather.*

Viburnum tinus *'Eve Price' is smaller and has a more compact shape than* V. tinus. *Its attractive pink buds open to faintest pink-tinged, well-scented flowers.*

Vinca - periwinkle

If you are looking for something to grow where almost nothing else will, *Vinca,* or periwinkle, is the plant to choose. This relaxed, rather sprawling ground cover plant, consists of lengths of sinewy stems clad in pairs of glossy, evergreen leaves that hug dry soil under trees, form low mounds or clamber into the lower branches of shrubs in a border. Although the periwinkle's star-shaped flowers have given their name to that particular shade of blue, there is also a white periwinkle and a mauve one; both green- and variegated-leaved forms of periwinkle are available with white flowers, but blue is still by far the most striking. Most attractive of all are the double-flowered forms occasionally available - and well worth seeking out. As well as tolerating 'difficult' dry soil situations in sun or shade, *Vinca* also grows fast enough to put up with the rough and tumble of a family garden and is useful for smothering out weeds. Planted on a bank with spring bulbs, periwinkle creates a good background to the flowers and a useful flowering and foliage feature for the rest of the year; it blooms all summer. It can be left on its own to colonize woodland floors, large shrub borders and bits of wild garden. The stems root as they run, so a colony is virtually self-perpetuating once established; you can dig up new plants at any time and move them. Where a 'tamer' periwinkle is needed, look for *Vinca minor* instead of the larger and faster *V. major.*

Above: Vinca major *tolerates poor soil and shady conditions, but if kept tidy makes a remarkably attractive plant, covered with flowers for most of the spring and summer.*

Above: V. difformis *flowers in the fall and early winter. In cold areas, stems are often killed to ground level in winter, but reappear the following year.*

Right: *Unlike many double-flowered plants, the blooms of* Vinca minor *'Flora Plena' are as weather-resistant as those of the single flower versions.*

Right: Vinca *produces two sorts of stems: leafy, upright ones that carry the flowers and long, wiry horizontal runners that root virtually anywhere they touch the soil. From each set of roots, new shoots appear that start a new plant. This in turn sends out more runners and soon you have a thicket.*

Tidying up vinca

If you want to keep vinca contained within a smaller space, no regular pruning is needed; just cut back long stems in spring and pull out those that have rooted where you do not want them. Where the plant has spread unchecked, you will need to clear through the many layers of stems that have built up over the years.

1 An overgrown periwinkle colony takes quite a bit of sorting out. Start by separating the wiry horizontal runners from the more upright leafy shoots that carry the flowers, and then cut out the long runners.

2 Remove the old dead stems and debris that have built up in the base of the plants, until you expose relatively clear soil around them.

3 Spread a mulch of 1-2in(2.5-5cm) of any well-rotted organic matter (such as old growing bag mixture or garden compost) around the plant.

4 This helps to restore the soil, which usually becomes heavily impoverished where a neglected carpet of periwinkle has run riot.

Right: Vinca minor 'Aureovariegata' combines a neat growth habit with variegated evergreen leaves and a long flowering season. It looks good even in poor growing conditions.

The tentacle-like runners are sent out in all directions and it is these that make periwinkles such good colonizers.

Weigela

Weigela are shrubs that deserve to rank high among the top ten, but are rather underrated, considering their many assets. They make elegant, arching, medium-sized bushes that flower profusely for about six weeks in early midsummer, producing large, open-ended, trumpet-shaped blooms in pink or red. The most spectacular varieties, however, are those that also have colorful foliage. *Weigela florida* 'Variegata' makes a very neat compact shrub about 4ft(1.2m) high, with striking cream-variegated leaves that look wonderful set against its pale pink flowers. *Weigela florida* 'Foliis Purpureis' (which looks superb planted with it) has bronze-purple leaves and bright pink flowers. It makes a slightly smaller plant, reaching about 3ft(90cm) high and the same across. All provide useful flowers and foliage for flower arranging. Weigelas are very undemanding shrubs to grow. They thrive in any reasonable garden soil, and do best in full sun, although they still perform in some slight shade. They do not need proper pruning as such, but to keep the plants looking neat, remove any unsightly brown, dead flowerheads. When all the flowers are over, cut back the old flowered stems to just beyond the last of the dead blooms. Combine weigelas in borders with other summer-flowering shrubs; the colored foliage kinds go very well with feathery hebe flowers. Or use them as a background for summer bulbs, such as the new orchid gladioli, or annual bedding plants. Single specimens of weigela make attractively shaped plants to grow on their own in the middle of a small lawn; the colored foliage kinds are particularly good in this situation.

Left: 'Evita' is a particularly good form of weigela, with deep wine-red flowers. Unfortunately, it is not very widely available; nurseries specializing in unusual shrubs may stock it.

Right: Weigelas look good with a wide range of companions in the garden. Here, Weigela florida 'Variegata' is growing with euphorbia, dicentra and Lamium maculatum against a background of conifers.

Pruning weigela

Weigelas tend to grow rather sparse and untidy unless regularly pruned after flowering. Dead-heading the plant and shortening the long stems also tidies the shape and encourages vigorous branching from the base, so that the plants stay bushy.

1 New plants from the nursery often benefit from a little inital shaping. This is quite a good example, with plenty of stems growing from the base, although there are a couple of straggly shoots.

Above: *The mauvey-pink flowers of Weigela florida 'Foliis Purpureis' make a good contrast with the purple foliage. Grow it in full sun so that the leaf color can develop fully.*

Below: *Paler flowered weigela can be charming, too; this apple-blossom pink one is 'Madame Couturier', but there are plenty of other cultivars. Team with brightly colored foliage.*

2 Cut very thin, whippy or out-of-shape shoots right back to their point of origin close to the base of the plant. Use sharp secateurs and avoid damaging the fragile young shoots clustered in the heart of the shrub.

3 The total removal of two stems has improved the shape. After flowering, cut all remaining stems to just below the lowest dead flowers to encourage shoots to develop from the center; they will carry the following year's flowers.

Index to Plants

90

Credits

The majority of the photographs featured in this book have been taken by Neil Sutherland and are © Colour Library Books. The publishers wish to thank the following photographers for providing additional photographs, credited here by page number and position on the page, i.e. (B)Bottom, (T)Top, (C)Center, (BL)Bottom left, etc.

Gillian Beckett: 43(BL), 48(TR), 65(T), 81(TL), 84(B)
Pat Brindley: 43(TL), 77(BR)
Eric Crichton: 10, 18(B), 19(TL,TR,B), 23(BR), 27(BR), 30(BL), 32(T), 33(T,BR), 34(TR,BR), 35(TL,TR), 39(BR), 42(BL,TR), 49(TL), 50(BR), 53(R), 54(TR), 55(BR), 57(TR,BL), 58(TL,BL), 59(L,BR), 60(BL,BR), 61(R), 67(TL,BL), 68(BL), 69(TL), 74(BL,BR), 75(TC), 77(TR), 78(BR), 79(TR), 80(BR), 82(L,TR,BR), 83(TL,BL), 86(TR), 87(BR), 88(R)
John Glover: Half title page, 18(T), 21(T), 28(L), 29(TR,BL), 31(CB,BR), 32(B), 37(T), 38(BR), 43(R), 45(TL), 51(BL), 52(B), 54(B), 65(BR), 67(TR), 69(BL,BR), 74(CR), 75(TR), 76(TR), 77(TL), 80(TR), 83(TR), 86(BL,BC)
S & O Mathews: 20(T), 23(CR), 31(L), 33(BL), 38-39(T), 39(BL), 44(B), 52(T), 55(BL), 56(BR), 57(BR), 58(BR), 66(TR), 75(TL), 77(BL), 79(L), 81(BL), 89(TR)
Clive Nichols: 28(BR, Designer Joan Murdy), 51(BR, Le Manoir Aux Quat Saisons, Oxfordshire), 53(TL, Little Bowden, Berkshire), 56(L), 59(TR), 61(BL), 85(TL, Carrog, Dyfed, Wales), 85(BL, Brook Cottage Garden, Oxfordshire)
Photos Horticultural: 27(TL), 36(B), 64(TR), 88(BL), 89(BR)

Acknowledgments

The publishers would like to thank the following people and organizations for their help during the preparation of this book: The Flower Auction Holland, Naaldwijk; Court Lane Nursery, Hadlow College, Kent; The Hillier Plant Center, Braishfield, Hampshire; The Sir Harold Hillier Gardens and Arboretum, Braishfield, Hampshire (managed and financed by Hampshire County Council); Murrells Nursery, Pulborough, West Sussex; Trehane Nursery, Wimborne, Dorset; Mike Warner-Horne.